FOREIGN

INVESTMENT

ADVISORY

SERVICE

Administrative Barriers to Foreign Investment

Reducing Red Tape

in Africa

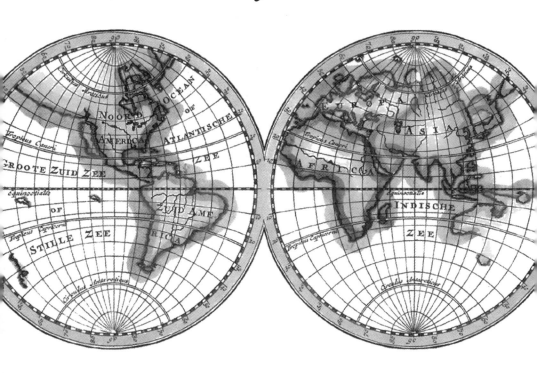

OCCASIONAL

PAPER

14

by
James J. Emery
Melvin T. Spence, Jr.
Louis T. Wells, Jr.
Timothy S. Buehrer

The International Finance Corporation (IFC), an affiliate of the World Bank, promotes the economic development of its member countries through investment in the private sector. It is the world's largest multilateral organization providing financial assistance directly in the form of loans and equity to private enterprises in developing countries.

The World Bank is a multilateral development institution whose purpose is to assist its developing member countries further their economic and social progress so that their people may live better and fuller lives.

The findings, interpretations, and conclusions expressed in this publication are those of the authors and do not necessarily represent the views and policies of the International Finance Corporation or the World Bank or their Boards of Executive Directors or the countries they represent. The IFC and the World Bank do not guarantee the accuracy of the data included in this publication and accept no responsibility whatsoever for any consequences of their use. Some sources cited in this paper may be informal documents that are not readily available.

The material in this publication is copyrighted. Requests for permission to reproduce portions of it should be sent to the General Manager, Foreign Investment Advisory Service (FIAS), at the address shown in the copyright notice above. FIAS encourages dissemination of its work and will normally give permission promptly and, when the reproduction is for noncommercial purposes, without asking a fee. Permission to copy portions for classroom use is granted through the Copyright Clearance Center, Inc., Suite 910, 222 Rosewood Drive, Danvers, Massachusetts 01923, U.S.A.

Library of Congress Cataloging-in-Publication Data has been applied for.

Contents

CUTTING RED TAPE: LESSONS FROM A CASE-BASED APPROACH TO IMPROVING THE INVESTMENT CLIMATE IN MOZAMBIQUE 95

Louis T. Wells, Jr., Timothy S. Buehrer

Figures and Tables

ADMINISTRATIVE BARRIERS TO INVESTMENT IN AFRICA

Figures

Tables

CUTTING RED TAPE: LESSONS FROM A CASE-BASED APPROACH TO IMPROVING THE INVESTMENT CLIMATE IN MOZAMBIQUE

Figures

Tables

Preface

For almost 15 years the Foreign Investment Advisory Service (FIAS), a joint service of the International Finance Corporation and the World Bank, has been helping governments in Africa to improve their environments for foreign direct investment (FDI). This advice has covered the basic rules governing FDI and the institutions that administer these rules. Many countries in Africa have been receptive to advice from FIAS and many other advisors, and have made substantial progress in improving the basic framework for FDI.

Yet, despite these improvements, FDI flows to Africa have continued to languish. In searching for the reasons for this stagnation FIAS and others have dug deeper into the investment environment and have uncovered a maze of second-order administrative barriers to the implementation and operations of investments. These barriers can affect both domestic and foreign private investors but they may have a disproportionate impact on foreign investors who usually have higher visibility and who tend to adhere more strictly to legal requirements.

The two papers in this volume provide an overview of administrative barriers in Africa, and a very in-depth look at how one country,

Mozambique, used a very large foreign investment as a mechanism to begin to tear them down. The first paper, co-authored by James Emery (a former FIAS staff member) is based on a series of country-specific studies on administrative barriers done by FIAS and the United States Agency for International Development. These studies covered Ghana, Mozambique, Namibia, Tanzania, and Uganda, and were completed in 1995–1997. Each country study relied on extensive research in the countries, including review of primary materials, laws, and regulations. References are not cited individually to the original source material or the country studies to avoid cumbersome and repetitive references to the same documents.

Because the original research on which the country studies are based is dated, there may be some inaccuracies in terms of the specific situations presented. Since the studies were completed and workshops held to discuss them, many improvements have already been made to address the constraints summarized in this paper. In that sense the picture portrayed here is somewhat unfair to the countries concerned as, in each case, they have made concrete improvements. Many areas remain untouched, however, and similar problems can be found in other countries, both within and outside the region. Where major changes have resulted, this has been noted in the text. The final chapter takes stock of some of the reforms countries have undertaken in response to the representation of unnecessary "red tape" in these analyses.

The second paper, by Professor Louis Wells of the Harvard Business School, is a detailed look at how the administrative barriers that existed in Mozambique threatened to derail the huge Mozal aluminum smelter that was proposed by South African investors. The size of the investment led the Government of Mozambique to find ways to deal with the administrative barriers. Not only were the barriers overcome for this special project but also the Government used the knowledge gained in the process to reduce barriers for all investors and establish institutions that could facilitate other investments. Perhaps most important, a cadre of bureaucrats emerged from the process with an appreciation of the damage that unnecessary red tape could do to the investment environment, and with a set of tools that could be used to facilitate future investments.

The message of both papers is that administrative barriers constitute a significant impediment to foreign direct investment in Africa. Moreover, many of the administrative procedures required of investors have no real justification. Nevertheless, removal of unnecessary barriers and streamlining other administrative procedures require very detailed efforts by governments involving the exercise of significant political leadership. An encouraging number of African governments are now engaged in this effort.

DALE R. WEIGEL
General Manager
Foreign Investment Advisory Service (FIAS)

Administrative Barriers to Investment in Africa

James J. Emery
Melvin T. Spence, Jr.

Acknowledgments

Financial support for the research and comparative data analysis in this report was provided by USAID through the Private Enterprise Development Support project.

Robert Rauth carried out the first of the FIAS country studies discussed in this report, a study of Ghana. He was also the primary author of the subsequent studies of Namibia, Tanzania, and Uganda. His extensive knowledge of business conditions in African countries and his passion for details and facts, together with his understanding of the role of government agencies in creating the "playing field" for free enterprise, led him naturally to focus on the types of administrative barriers to investment discussed in this paper. He developed the approach examined here and became a powerful advocate for the importance of paying attention to the realities faced by private businesses, large and small, foreign and local. He was able to use this type of detailed information to press effectively for reforms at all levels, from revising fundamental legislation to setting up a customer service window for investors at the municipal government offices in Windhoek, Namibia. And he was able to be sharply critical of bureaucratic procedures and red tape while still retaining the respect of officials responsible for administering the systems. His untimely death in 1997 has left all of those who worked with him and knew him with a sincere loss. His contributions to this work continue to guide those who have followed in his steps.

Acronyms

CMA	Common Monetary Area (southern Africa)
FDI	Foreign Direct Investment
FIAS	Foreign Investment Advisory Service
LIBOR	London Interbank Offered Rate
PEC	Public Employment Centers
SACU	South African Customs Union
UEB	Uganda Electricity Board
USAID	United States Agency for International Development

Executive Summary

With the hope of promoting private sector development, countries across sub-Saharan Africa have undertaken a sweeping change of policy in the past decade to liberalize and open their economies. To varying degrees, attention has been focused on areas such as

- Creating a stable macroeconomic environment;
- Liberalizing controls on foreign exchange transactions;
- Liberalizing price, licensing, and other controls on both domestic markets and international trade;
- Rationalizing tax and tariff structures, including reduction of average rates;
- Liberalizing investment laws and restrictions; and
- Actively promoting foreign investment and exports.

Despite these and other improvements, however, the formal investment response in most countries has been disappointing. At the same time, micro and informal enterprises are not only failing to "graduate" to the formal sector, but are playing an increasingly important commercial role. As a result, African governments are becoming increasingly skeptical regarding the effectiveness of economic liberalization—particularly because many senior-level officials believe that the reform process has been largely completed.

Even in countries that have addressed constraints to private investment and exports, significant deterrents remain. In particular, countries with a long history of government intervention and administrative direction over economic decisions typically have complex, overlapping controls beyond those easily identified as constraints on investment or addressed at a macro level by the types of policy reforms mentioned above. The persistence of these "second-tier" administrative barriers to investment, combined with a lack of institutional capacity in the government agencies responsible for them, often translates into a situation where these mere procedural tasks become major obstacles to investment. Such difficulties can often be overcome only after long delays or with extraordinary payments. This discourages investors, even many who may have made a preliminary decision to commit to a country. "One-stop shops," established by countries throughout Africa to streamline investment procedures, have also been a big disappointment: few have actually improved the situation and some have made it worse. The reality, then, is often far removed from the incantations of government officials that they are now "open and friendly" to private investors. All too many developing countries still need more comprehensive reform efforts, combined with radical overhauls of the way in which their government agencies operate.

At an implementation level, many officials remain distrustful of private businesspeople, or at least view them simply as a source of supplemental income generation. Both views can mean the persistence of otherwise lower-level irritants to business formation and operation, a persistence that often magnifies the irritants to the point of constraints in an overall investment climate that remains hostile. In many cases the "old" attitudes still prevail among bureaucrats, who assert their authority through less direct controls, such as their ability to interrupt business operations for otherwise routine clearances, inspections, or verifications. In this environment, existing private businesses commonly complain of administrative "harassment."

Methodology

This paper draws on studies of administrative barriers to investment in five African countries that FIAS and USAID have studied: Ghana, Mozambique, Namibia, Tanzania, and Uganda. Following a similar methodology, the studies identified all the steps required to undertake an investment, from registering a company to starting operations, in full compliance with existing laws and regulations.[1] This report presents an overview of the types of obstacles encountered and the resulting effects in terms of a negative impact on the investment climate. These obstacles are grouped into four categories:

1. General approvals and licenses required of all firms,
2. Specialized or sectoral approvals required of firms in particular sectors,
3. Requirements to gain access to land for business facilities, and
4. Licenses or other requirements once firms are operational.

General Approvals, Licenses, and Registrations

A number of steps are typically required of all firms trying to establish a new business. In some countries, such as Mozambique, simply registering a company can be a long and expensive process; in others, such as Uganda, it is theoretically easy, but outmoded legislation and a registrar general's office with no resources have made it unnecessarily cumbersome. The greatest obstacles and delays have occurred with countries that license investments and award fiscal incentives for qualifying firms (typically those in sectors viewed as development priorities). Here the need to prepare detailed feasibility studies and demonstrate project compliance with (often vague) eligibility criteria pose additional burdens on firms and frequently cause delays long exceeding legal time limits. Business licenses, often at a local level, are another source of delays and duplicative submission of company and project data. For foreign firms, special registration requirements for foreign investors are common, and significant delays are encountered in securing work permits for investors and expatriate managers. Duplicative tax registration procedures are common as well. As a result, these initial hurdles can often take many months, or even a year in some countries for complex projects.

Specialized Approvals

An additional layer of government scrutiny and evaluation of projects is applied for certain sectors, of which this report addresses industry, fisheries, forestry, and tourism.[2] Here, although concession procedures are particularly non-transparent, the awarding of concessions is the primary policy tool for resource management. As a result, effective resource management policies are often undermined and optimum levels of investment and exploitation are usually not reached. Governments also extend sectoral regulation into many areas. They might prescribe management structures and qualifications requirements for tourism companies, for example, or limit foreign investment, often in contradiction with stated policy in other laws.

Requirements to Gain Access to Land, Site Development, and Utility Connections

It is when buying or leasing land, constructing facilities, and securing utilities services that investors encounter the greatest delays. Undeveloped markets in private real estate mean that reliance on public sector land is virtually a necessity. Unfortunately, poor policy formulation, cumbersome and non-transparent procedures for making land available for commercial use, and tenure rights for informal occupants often make for a long and uncertain process for investors. Before investors can develop land and construct commercial or industrial facilities, they must obtain a series of approvals and licenses. Here again, significant delays can be encountered and the responsible authorities are often poorly equipped to evaluate proposed plans. Securing connections to utility services—power, water and sewer, and telephone—is also fraught with delays. New connections may be impossible in some areas, or the cost of extension must be borne entirely by the investor. Due to a lack of new capacity, finding a fully serviced site in a desirable location can be quite difficult; this was true across all the countries surveyed.

These are significant, systemic problems stemming from years of neglect and mismanagement, and cannot be overcome easily. Although some countries are proceeding with privatization of utilities or private participation in infrastructure sectors, progress has been slow and concrete results have yet to be realized.

Operational Requirements

Once operational, companies face a different series of interactions with government agencies. These are typically regulations and controls on foreign trade, foreign exchange, and labor and social security. These areas are often the source of license or permit requirements that remain cumbersome in spite of overall liberalization. There is still progress to be made in adapting former control-oriented institutions to a role of selective monitoring and enforcement.

Conclusion: The Red Tape Analysis

When added together, this whole maze of often duplicative, complex, and non-transparent procedures can mean delays of up to two years to get investments approved and operational. The red tape has its origins in outdated procedures, inappropriate policies, poor implementation, and a lack of institutional capacity in government agencies. It is often reflected in the inability of organizations to implement fully their mandates and is typically circumvented, often with payments, to ensure the compliance of government officials.

Because barriers to investment cover a broad range of policy, administrative, and institutional areas, reducing or removing them can be a daunting task. Measures that have had some effect in the countries analyzed here have included an open and frank discussion between public and private sectors, initiated by the presentation of the studies undertaken. Following this, support by donor agencies in the form of targeted technical assistance to agencies showing a particular interest in reforms has proven useful.

Ultimately, this external support may be combined with more substantial resources in a capacity-building effort. The latter can only be effective, however, once a change of attitude has occurred in the agency, a change that would include the introduction of a "customer service" ethic. Although tackling these barriers is difficult, it can be done. In the countries studied, as well as in others, substantial improvements have been made in a relatively short time.

1

Introduction

Economic reforms, which have been carried out for more than a decade, have been supplemented by political changes with the aim of promoting a social dialogue, to create a lawful state with a pluralist democracy . . . . [Our country] is now a safe haven for investors. . . . We have clearly opted for the promotion of a market economy based on a free-trade system, viewing the private sector as the driving force for economic growth. . . . In order to facilitate the creation of enterprises, the Government has set up a One-Stop-Shop system for the quick processing of dossiers to allow the creation of an enterprise in 72 hours.

—Investment promotion literature for an African country

Productive investment levels in most African countries have remained depressed, and even where economic policy reform has been implemented, the investor response—both domestic and foreign—has been poor.

—World Bank policy research paper

I've been here for a year now getting a simple business started. At every turn, there is a new twist, a new person with his hand out for a payment, and a new requirement nobody told me about. It took me most of that time to get a site and get utility connections; I'm still waiting for a phone. There is always a law or a regulation that says something I'm doing is illegal, but I never find out about it until they show up at my door with a notice.

—A foreign investor

9

These three quotations illustrate varying perspectives on the climate for investment in sub-Saharan Africa. They could have come from virtually any of the countries in the region. Although at first they may seem conflicting, the three statements are not mutually exclusive. Rather, they point out what will be presented as the central theme of this paper: that although substantial liberalization and reforms have occurred in investment policy as well as other areas and although most countries now unabashedly promote themselves as investment sites, the reality facing investors on the ground is far different. The third quotation above—actually a composite from many interviews with investors in the region—illustrates the frustration many firms and entrepreneurs have felt when, having made an initial decision to invest in a country, they are faced with the many hurdles, delays, inadequate public services, and procedural requirements standing in the way of starting a business. Although this perspective alone cannot explain the "lack of investor response" that has characterized Africa and preoccupied analysts from development institutions, it certainly accounts for a great deal of what is wrong with investment climates in Africa.

This paper examines administrative constraints to investment in a series of African countries, based on the experience of advisory projects undertaken in Ghana, Namibia, Uganda, Mozambique and Tanzania.[3]

Liberalization and Reform

Sub-Saharan Africa has experienced the beginnings of an economic turnaround in the second half of the 1990s. Reversing a trend since the late 1970s, the region has realized positive real growth in GDP per capita over a sustained period from 1995 to 1997; excluding oil producers and South Africa, this trend continued into 1998. Most countries on the continent have substantially liberalized their economies since the 1980s, the result being a greater reliance on (1) market mechanisms in lieu of direct state intervention and (2) the private sector as the engine for growth. This liberalization has in part been a response to pressure and assistance through adjustment lending from the World Bank and International Monetary Fund (IMF). But it has also been a pragmatic response to worsening economic conditions, the obvious failures of most features of the statist model, and the need for drastic new measures to achieve economic progress. Broadly speaking, the objective of these reforms has been to promote private sector development, attract new private investment, and restore economic growth.

To varying degrees, these policy reforms have been focused on areas such as

- *Creating a stable macroeconomic environment* by controlling public sector deficits, restraining money supply growth, and financing deficits from capital markets or aid flows, all of which contribute to low inflation, stable exchange rates, and positive real interest rates in financial markets;
- *Freeing domestic markets* by ending price controls, profit margin ceilings, subsidies, and other market interventions that had distorted incentives for and returns to private firms;
- *Liberalizing controls on foreign exchange transactions* by removing administrative controls on current transactions, using market mechanisms to determine exchange rates, allowing foreign exchange accounts, and fostering the role of commercial banks and foreign exchange bureaus as the main market participants;
- *Liberalizing trade,* including ending most import and export licensing, reducing and simplifying tariffs, refraining from the use of quotas and other non-tariff barriers, introducing export promotion schemes (e.g., duty remission, drawback, bonded warehouses, and export processing zones), and removing export taxes;
- *Rationalizing tax structures* by reducing the highest marginal rates and expanding direct tax bases, introducing value-added taxes, and improving enforcement and administration;
- *Liberalizing private investment* by reforming restrictive investment legislation, opening sectors reserved for the state or nationals, removing advance approval requirements, guaranteeing equal treat-

ment for foreign investors, providing fiscal incentives for new investment, signing bilateral investment treaties and multilateral conventions, establishing "one-stop approval centers," and establishing investment promotion organizations; and

■ *Reforming the financial sector* by removing controls on interest rates, ending directed lending, promoting trading in government debt instruments in secondary markets, establishing equity markets, and encouraging foreign portfolio investment.

Because of these reforms, the climate for private investment and the general economic health of most African countries has greatly improved. However, reform implementation has been inconsistent and has not, in general, led to a resumption of the type of broad-based economic growth that both addresses poverty alleviation and provides an attraction for private investors. Certain reviews of the structural adjustment experience point out the need for deeper, broader reforms, stating in effect that the countries have not gone far enough.[4] Other analyses have pointed to the need for (1) carefully sequenced reforms introduced over a period of time and (2) a focus on institutional development to complement policy changes and ensure their effective implementation.[5] Harsher critics of these reforms have decried their consequences in terms of a reduction in public spending, introduction of competition, exposure to global trade and financial "shocks," and the unquestioning promotion of private investment and market-oriented economic policies.[6]

Even in their partial effectiveness, these reforms have nevertheless made a tremendous difference in restoring, or creating from ground zero, a business climate that is more attractive to private investors. Without the reforms there would have been a continuation of a small, closed private sector characterized by the type of protected, high-profit, short-term business ventures that depend on patronage and typify most unstable economies. In that environment, if successful, businesses typically generated only capital flight rather than increased investment.

Although the experience with implementation of these reforms has been uneven across Africa, in virtually every case—successful or not, they have been accompanied by earnest anticipation of dramatically increased private investment flows. In some cases, reform programs were accompanied by investment promotion efforts aimed at foreign investors, nationals, and expatriate nationals. In general, these flows have not materialized.

The Lack of Investor Response

This lack of response by private investors to the more open (and, presumably, more attractive) environment has occasioned much debate. In response to the more open environment, many private businessmen, foreign and domestic, began to make serious efforts at making their firms more competitive, after years of languishing (often profitably) in protected markets. At the same time as they began to make these efforts, they were also subjected to increased competition, primarily from imports and declining profitability. The risk environment changed and now called for a more challenging type of management and entrepreneurial skills that many firms did not possess. Businessmen successful in operating in protected environments and profiting from rent seeking proved to be less skilled, and less interested, in competing in a more open marketplace.

Nor have those flows come from new foreign investors. Sub-Saharan Africa remains marginal in terms of global investment flows, largely missing out on the tremendous expansion of foreign direct investment (FDI) in developing countries that has happened during the last decade. Although the absolute levels of foreign investment have increased modestly, Africa's share of developing-country FDI inflows decreased to 3.8 percent in 1996, its lowest levels since the early 1980s.[7] This meager performance is further tempered by the fact that FDI in Africa remains concentrated in resource extraction industries, which are driven more by resource endowments, extraction costs, and world market oil and mineral prices than the competitiveness of the local economy. Although some countries such as Ghana, Côte d'Ivoire, and Uganda have seen higher flows of FDI outside the extractive sectors, these flows are still quite small by most absolute and relative measures. They do not approach the magnitudes of fast-growing countries in other regions where growth has been paced by FDI.

The one area of the private sector that has undeniably flourished with liberalization is the informal sector. Here, fueled at least partially by trade liberalization and the easy availability of consumer goods at lower prices, small-scale traders and marginal service vendors have become one of the few dynamic forces adapting well to the new, more open market economies of Africa. Their formal-sector competitors denounce the swelling ranks of street vendors, market stalls, kiosks, and small shops for not paying taxes and avoiding business regulation. However, against expectations, informal sector firms that prosper not only fail to graduate to the formal sector but seem to encourage more entrants in their wake. And yet, the proliferation of the informal sector is undeniably a natural market-driven response to current conditions: the environment is still too risky for large investments; it is expensive to be licensed, pay taxes, and comply with rules; and there is the ever-present potential for downstream policy reversals to change the rules of the game.

The disappointing results have been noted by officials from those governments that introduced reforms. Very often they took substantial political risks to do so, relying on the promise of new investments and rapid growth to alleviate the short-term dislocations from such reforms. As a result, skepticism over the effectiveness of economic liberalization is becoming more widespread, particularly because many senior level officials believe that the reform process has been largely completed. To generate domestic political support these leaders sometimes decry the imposed mandates of the World Bank and IMF, further undermining the effectiveness of reform programs.

Among analysts, the relative paucity of new investment flows has firmly entered the lexicon as *the lack of a supply response*. Debates now center on the impact of these reform programs, their "depth" and speed, and how they can be managed differently in the future to ensure more positive results.[8] Yet irrespective of this debate, no one will deny that in most African countries problems remain in the investment climates that affect the "supply response" of investors. This paper is not concerned with determining whether this is a result of reforms not having gone far enough, institutional weakness, or inadequate pacing of reforms and support in implementation. Rather, we focus on the existing array of regulations and bureaucratic requirements that confront investors and how these administrative constraints continue to deter new investment.

Administrative Barriers to Investment

There are clearly a variety of factors behind Africa's continued failure to attract productive private investment. This paper makes the simple proposition that a large part of the problem, at least in terms of the paucity of new investment, can be found by looking at the actual experience that confronts investors when they set up a company. In particular, this experience too often consists of a morass of licenses, approvals, permits, and other requirements that result in undue delays and unforeseen costs, encourage bribery and corruption, and foster an environment of pervasive uncertainty for all investors. These administrative constraints to investment, which often have their origins in the earlier era of extensive state control over private investment, persist in spite of a substantial opening-up of the economy. Although the restrictive policies may have changed, the institutions that implemented them still exist and the procedures they spawned persist or even proliferate.

Let us put aside for the moment the deterrents to investment arising from questions of comparative advantage, resource endowments, factor costs, transportation links, and most of the other fundamentals that determine investor flows. The bottom line is that in most African countries the procedures for setting up a company and entering into legitimate business are a nightmare. When someone has finally made the decision to invest he then is subjected to some of the worst treatment imaginable, sometimes from the various agencies of that government that so actively courted him in the first place. In a few cases this treatment consists of outright extortion: presenting the investor with insurmountable delays or repeated obstacles unless he makes a large payoff or gives a shareholding to a "friend" in the government or to his or her relative.

In most cases, however, the types of obstacles encountered are more mundane. Although these procedural requirements may invoke graft as a means of dealing with the situation, this is typically on a petty scale. These types of procedural hurdles include

- Registering a company
- Securing investment incentives
- Securing sectoral or other business licensing
- Getting a tax number
- Documenting the investment to be made (for foreign investors)
- Leasing, purchasing, or otherwise gaining access to land
- Getting utilities services connected
- Securing work permits for expatriate managers
- Obtaining building permits and municipal licenses
- Importing equipment and inputs
- Having health and safety inspections performed
- Complying with employment formalities.

The maintenance of overly complex registration procedures, combined with a lack of institutional capacity, often means that these mere procedural tasks become major obstacles to investment.

At lower levels of bureaucracy, officials are often still distrustful of private businessmen. Alternatively, businessmen are simply viewed as a source of supplemental income generation for underpaid and dispirited bureaucrats. Both motivations can mean the persistence of otherwise lower-level irritants to business formation and operation, often elevating them to the point of constraints in an overall investment climate that remains hostile. This has been true notwithstanding a commitment to reform and liberalization at decision-making levels of government. These factors can be particularly negative for foreign investors who may not be politically connected, operate under strict internal corporate guidelines, or do not have local partners to take care of the multitude of procedural obstacles and associated payments.

There are a number of symptoms associated with this degree of administrative complexity, in terms of how it affects both private investment and private sector development overall. Indications that second-tier administrative constraints are a problem include the following:

■ *Rigid and pervasive barriers between formal and informal sectors.* Although not the only element encouraging the growth of the informal sector, administrative complexity is certainly a contributing factor. Regulatory compliance, as much as paying taxes, can increase the cost of becoming a formal sector enterprise.

■ *Very little 100-percent–foreign investment.* Foreign investors often rely on local partners or intermediaries to negotiate the maze of requirements and payoffs required to establish a business. In practice, few foreign firms decide to go it alone, even though that might be their preference.

■ *Low implementation rates for new investment projects.* Although there are many reasons why new projects are abandoned, very low rates of realization for new investment projects are an indicator of severe problems encountered by firms as they try to proceed. Some countries, such as Ghana, have had an implementation rate of less than 20 percent among firms registering new investments.[9]

■ *Reliance on screening versus monitoring and enforcement.* In most African countries, governments have relied on up-front screening and controls over investment as a means of regulating economic activity, rather than monitoring and enforcement of actual actions by firms once they are operational. Even where general investment licensing may have been abandoned, other types of licenses and approvals are typically required. This reflects in part institutional weakness and an inability to enforce regulations on operating businesses.

■ *Corruption.* Corruption, whether on a small or grand scale, is facilitated by the various types of administrative constraints and procedural requirements on investors. Where these choke points have proliferated, so have the opportunities for extracting payments from businesses. Where corruption is endemic, there is a further uncertainty associated with the discretionary authority of officials in applying the maze of regulations.

■ *Poor relations between the public and private sectors.* Relations between government and the private sector are often strained and not productive in this type of environment. Government officials may consider businessmen simply as plotting to evade taxes and other responsibilities, opportunistically as sources of bribes, or cynically as benefitting from protection or other advantages accorded by them. Businessmen, on the other hand, may feel that governments have no respect for the risks they take, act capriciously with no regard for business interests, and simply look to them as sources of money, whether for taxes, political contributions, or bribes. Excessive regulation in fact fosters these kinds of behavior on both sides, producing the very actions it is supposedly meant to curb.

These symptoms are quite widespread in Africa, and reflect a number of other influences besides administrative complexity and over-regulation. However, their presence is also a good indicator that there are regulatory issues and administrative constraints affecting the investment environment, compounding what may be an already weak picture in terms of economic fundamentals.

The Analytical Approach

FIAS began confronting these issues at the outset of its efforts to advise African nations on improving the investment climate. Initially, most FIAS advisory projects focused on the major policy issues affecting the investment environment as well as the restrictiveness of specific investment regimes or codes. After more than a decade of experience with African liberalization and improvements in the general investment climate, however, secondary factors increasingly emerged as major constraints and typified the actual experience of firms attempting to invest, which complained of all the obstacles in their paths.

FIAS' attention to these matters was at first neither systematic nor well defined in terms of an analytical approach. As a result, early attempts to focus policy makers' attention on these issues were often rebuffed. For example, a 1991 study on Côte d'Ivoire documented the 61 discrete steps required to establish a business, in order to illustrate this type of problem.[10] In subsequent work in 1995 in Ghana a more coherent methodology was established and further refined in the following years in Namibia, Mozambique, Tanzania, and Uganda by FIAS and The Services Group.[11]

This methodology is quite simple. It consists of documenting in precise detail all the administrative requirements for establishing a business and making it operational. This includes all licenses, approvals, registrations, permits, or other formalities required to be in full compliance with existing laws and regulations. In addition, project teams also gathered data on the delays associated with each step, the costs, and the forms or information required. This research was typically done in full collaboration with government agencies whose active participation in the process was solicited from the beginning. As an example of this methodology, Figure 1 illustrates graphically the steps in the process for a foreign manufacturing firm in Uganda.

Once the administrative and logistical hurdles of making an investment are mapped out as in Figure 1, it is easy to identify areas of duplication, excessively complex and intrusive requirements, or ineffectual implementation. The recommendations made for each country typically focus on areas where administrative procedures can be simply eliminated, streamlined, or otherwise improved to ensure that they are not constraints. Where regulatory controls or informational requirements are maintained, recommendations often emphasize improving implementation. This often means changing the attitude of government agencies from one of control and distrust to one of service provision and facilitation, along with ensuring compliance.

FIGURE 1
Steps for a Foreign Manufacturing Operation in Uganda

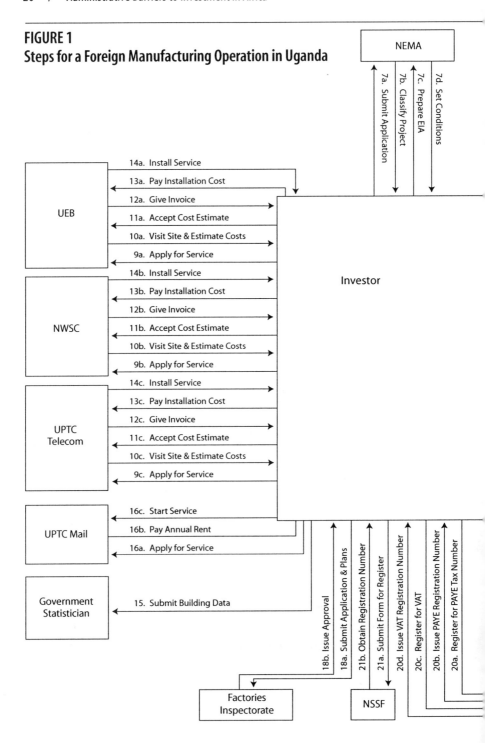

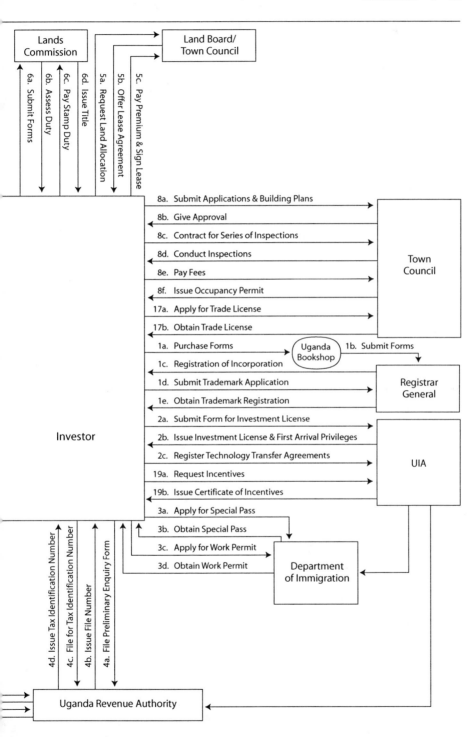

Antecedents

In terms of documenting the types of procedures, this approach is itself not new; much related work has also focused on the impact on businesses of the legal, regulatory, and institutional environment. A major contribution was made by the work of Hernando de Soto who, in his 1987 work *The Other Path*, dramatized the Byzantine regulatory obstacles to small, informal sector firms in Peru by describing the distance one has to travel to attend to all the required formalities, and the attendant delays.[12] De Soto's focus, however, was on the informal sector and the need to increase access by small-scale businesses to formal sector benefits such as property rights and access to credit.

A number of studies have attempted, often via surveys, to identify constraints to investment or obstacles to business expansion. Some, including those that focus on Africa, have generally tended to downplay the role of regulatory constraints as constraints on investment. Surveys of African businesses undertaken by the World Bank's Regional Program for Enterprise Development have shown that regulatory issues rank relatively low in terms of constraints on growth at the firm level.[13] However, at a disaggregated level, these issues ranked relatively higher for larger firms and for those in certain sectors. Other enterprise surveys undertaken for the 1997 World Development Report showed quite a bit of difference by region. In Africa, regulatory constraints *per se* (including those related to starting a business) were low on the list, with corruption, taxes, and infrastructure the most important.[14] The same authors, in an empirical study of institutional factors affecting investment, found that indicators of corruption and lack of rule of law had the strongest effect on differential investment rates among developing countries.[15]

These surveys and empirical studies point to some of the same assertions that will be developed here. It is clear that there are obstacles to investment in Africa—such as political instability, weak infrastructure, and poor economic performance—that constitute more fundamental constraints on investment than administrative, institutional, or regulatory constraints. However, for those investors who still decide to pursue projects in African countries these other obstacles come into play and often frustrate the implementation of their projects.

Another approach attempts to quantify the impact of these kind of administrative and regulatory constraints in terms of the increase in transaction costs to firms. In this approach, detailed enterprise surveys of selected samples of firms are used to gather data concerning delays, managerial time, and other sources of increased costs associated with these types of constraints.[16] This work represents an evolving methodology that has the potential for providing some rigorous estimates of the added costs of these types of obstacles for investment and business expansion.

From a different perspective, the recent literature on "reinventing government" has also attempted to focus on the nature of business regulation and the impact of government bureaucracies on private sector growth. Here the focus is from the perspective of improving government performance and, in particular, shifting the focus of government programs to emphasize service delivery and the extension of private sector management principles to public services, often by innovative methods of private provision of services. Although there has been some attention at the national level in the U.S.,[17] the thrust of the movement has been at the state and municipal levels.[18] Yet this perspective, while relevant to the improvement of many public services in Africa and developing countries, does not focus squarely on the problems created in the investment climate. This experience, although concentrated in the developed countries, is nonetheless relevant to developing countries in terms of lessons to be learned from different approaches to improving government services.

The initiatives summarized here all in various ways support and complement the focus of the approach developed in this paper. The main difference is that this approach has focused on analyzing the nature and extent of these bureaucratic procedures themselves. In this respect, the work conducted to date has gone much farther than general surveys inquiring about regulatory obstacles and as a result can offer much more specific policy recommendations for addressing the issues. It is complementary to empirical and quantitative studies that have attempted to assess the magnitude of these constraints, either through the cost to individual firms or in the resulting investment flows. The approach developed here can have a much greater impact in dealing with some of the inertia and reluctance to change that often characterizes bureaucratic behavior, by relying on detailed assessment of procedures and administrative requirements.

Administrative Constraints in Sub-Saharan Africa

These second-tier policy and administrative constraints are not unique to Africa. Other regions, including Latin America and the Middle East, suffer from many related problems in the investment climate. However, the problem is perhaps most consistently displayed among sub-Saharan African countries and the route by which they got there is, for the most part, different. In Africa, the degree of administrative complexity is quite directly related to the post-colonial interventionist policies pursued by those countries and, in some cases, to carry-overs from the colonial era itself. Colonial regimes often imposed complex regulations to protect the position of firms from the home country and limit the areas where local businesses could operate. On top of this legal basis were grafted a host of administrative controls to ensure governmental primacy over private businesses for the newly independent nations which were, overwhelmingly, run by ex-colonials. This economic nationalism extended to a socialist orientation in most countries, meaning direct government ownership of most formal-sector economic organizations and strict controls over private economic activity. With liberalization, much of this structure has been done away with; however, many of the institutions survive, along with their procedures and requirements, even though today they may serve little purpose.

The following chapters investigate the nature of these administrative constraints to investment for a group of countries in which these types of studies have been completed and data is available. The chapters are divided into four areas, roughly corresponding to the chronological process of making an investment:

■ General licenses, approvals, and other requirements for all firms, including general investment approval, approvals for incentives, tax registration, company formation, expatriate work permits, and business licenses;

■ Specialized approvals required for certain sectors or activities such as are typically required for sectors involving resource utilization, tourism, financial services, and transportation;

■ Site development constraints, encompassing securing land, improving it, getting utilities services, and constructing buildings; and

■ Operational requirements—the result of regulations governing such areas as labor, foreign exchange, international trade, and standards—that firms must meet once they begin operations.

2

General Approvals, Licenses, and Registrations

A ll governments in sub-Saharan Africa require investors to carry
out a certain number of administrative steps. These typically include registering a company or business name, securing work permits and residence visas for foreign investors and expatriate
employees, registering with the tax authorities and other agencies,
getting general business licenses, and getting access to investment
incentives or other benefits that may be available under the investment law or other legislation.

In some cases the requirements involve applications that are
evaluated; in others they are simple registrations. In most cases
there is little regulatory control to be exercised and it is at this
stage where countries focus much of their efforts on expediting
procedures for investors and where investment promotion agencies have a strong role. Some have established one-stop shops for
investment approval, others guarantee maximum times for approvals, and still others have eliminated most prior approvals and require only a "simple registration."

Despite these efforts, however, major sources of delay and frustration for investors remain in all the countries analyzed. Although

the red tape varies significantly in nature and origin from country to country, its existence points to the need for continued reform as well as promotional and facilitation measures.

Company Registration

The first step in pursuing any investment is often to register a company. Other steps, such as prior approvals required under existing investment legislation, may be initiated first or may require having a company established in order to apply. This process is straightforward in most countries of the world and simply involves documenting the capital structure of the company, its form under the alternatives available in the "companies law," and recording of other pertinent details. Supporting documentation may be required (e.g., a resolution from the parent company) but little scrutiny is given except to satisfy informational and compliance needs and to ensure that the company or business name is not already in use.

Nevertheless, in Africa registering a company can be time-consuming. Complications were found in all the countries examined, as follows:

■ In Uganda no forms were available from the registrar general's office—the office had no money for printing—although they were available from a local bookstore. The office was not computerized and records were haphazard. Seven different forms were required, some of which were duplicative; and they had to be filed in several distinct steps.

■ In Ghana, as well, the registrar's office had no forms although a few individuals would loan their personal copy for a fee to be copied by investors.

■ In Namibia the number of forms required (an average of 10) and restrictiveness of the Companies Act leads most new investors to use the Close Corporation Act, which was designed to facilitate small and micro-enterprise formalization. That act, however, is still too demanding for those groups (even if it is attractive to larger formal-sector firms). Women are required to have their husband's written consent to form a company.

■ In all countries except Mozambique (that is, the former British colonies with registrars general or the equivalent) there was no facility for registration outside the capital. Businessmen located in the provinces were required to travel there with all the required documentation and then wait up to a week or more to receive the registration confirmation. As a result, only major businesses from outside the capital bothered to register.

It is in Mozambique, however, that the process of company formation was the most expensive, complicated, and prolonged. As is common in civil code countries, it is mandatory to have company statutes prepared by an accredited *notaire*, whose fees range up to 2.5 percent of capital. One-half of the capital for closely held companies must be placed in a bank account prior to registration (10 percent for limited liability companies). With the addition of registration fees, notary fees, and other required payments, the total cost of registering a company typically approaches 10 percent of capital.

Furthermore, a large amount of corroborating material is required, especially for foreign shareholders, so that assembling the registration package can take time and the process can be put on hold by rejection for lack of supporting documentation. Company statutes must be published in the *Official Gazette* as part of the process. In all, it can easily take up to six months just to register a company. This compares poorly to the two-to-five day performance of the other countries in the region.[19]

Foreign Investment Registration

In addition to the requirements for registering a company, countries typically require a separate registration for foreign investments. Ghana, Mozambique, Namibia, Tanzania, and Uganda all require this step; it is reportedly for informational purposes and is accomplished via an investment promotion agency. However, this was not a major problem in any of the countries studied: it was just another required step, albeit one that was probably unnecessary. The same information could be captured in the process of company registration, with information provided to the relevant agency by the registrar of companies or by the tribunal.

In Mozambique and Uganda, additional information is required of foreign shareholders in the registration process, which can be time-consuming. This includes police records, employment visas or work permits, and translations of parent company statutes or articles as well as resolutions authorizing the subsidiary in question. These steps often increased the time and effort associated with company registration.[20] In Ghana and Uganda, minimum capital requirements for foreign investment require further documentation and verification, which is either done as part of the registration process or in terms of certifying the award of incentives.

It is noteworthy that, with the exception of small negative lists in the investment laws of each country and minimum capital requirements (often higher for trading or commercial activity), the countries in this group are quite open to foreign investment. Although there are often secondary obstacles such as those in sectoral legislation or associated with access to land and finance (see Chapter 4), the overall policy stance of these countries is relatively open. This reflects the general trend worldwide toward fewer restrictions on foreign direct investment.[21]

Few countries maintain differential incentives for foreign investors. One is Uganda, which accords them and expatriate employees "first arrival privileges," in which a vehicle for personal use and other personal effects may be brought in with no duty payments. Although these privileges are attractive to foreign investors (especially given the high duty rates on vehicles) they require the cumbersome approval of both the Investment Authority and Customs.

Otherwise, all the investment laws of the countries concerned contain both "equal treatment" clauses that (1) guarantee foreign firms equal treatment with nationals and (2) guarantee foreign investors the rights of profit remittance and capital repatriation.

Access to Investment Incentives

Of the five countries, Mozambique, Namibia, and Uganda have systems of investment incentives available only to qualifying firms, as defined under special legislation. Intended to be an attraction for investors, in their application these programs have proved problematical. In contrast, Ghana and Tanzania have each, in relatively recent reforms, done away with approval-based incentives requiring screening and evaluation of investment projects. In so doing they have simplified tremendously the process of investment.[22]

The problems can be summarized by examining the incentives Uganda provides under its Investment Code:[23]

■ Applicants must first establish a company and prepare a business plan or feasibility study. That study must demonstrate compliance with the law in terms of minimum value-added requirements, minimum capital requirements, employment of nationals, and so on.

■ This plan or study is reviewed at three separate levels within the Uganda Investment Authority—staff, management, and board. This normally takes up to six weeks, depending on the scheduling of management and board meetings.

■ There are varying levels of incentive (for example, length of tax holiday) that are based on satisfaction of differing requirements. These must be determined from the application. Additional documentation is required for non-standard duty exemptions.

■ Once approved, incentives are not automatically enacted; the investor must demonstrate achievement of the minimum investment levels, based on an audit of qualifying assets. Only then is a Certificate of Incentives authorizing the tax exemptions prepared for transmission to the tax authorities.

■ Once the certificate is in place there are still questions about booking depreciation, the carry-forward of losses during the tax holiday period, and other important points that are only beginning to be sorted out.

The award of incentives in Uganda was seen as something extraordinary that had to be carefully evaluated and documented. Although this may in some sense have been necessary to prevent fraud, it also increased the burden on investors in terms of the preparation of feasibility studies, delays in processing applications, and uncertainty over final valuations. The administrative headaches of this relatively simple system of tax holidays was one of the main reasons the country has moved to eliminate them in favor of more automatic tax allowances for new investment, administered by the tax authorities through the tax code.

In Mozambique a similar problem exists in terms of (1) requirements for feasibility studies and supporting documentation from investors and (2) the screening process of the Center for Investment Promotion. Delays were common and requests for additional information frequent. Officials often asked questions regarding the financial projections, despite the policy statement that financial performance was the concern of the investor rather than the government.

It is ironic, but increasingly realized by governments and their promotion agencies, that these systems of administered tax holidays are in fact *dis*incentives. Established as an important benefit to bestow upon qualifying investors, in their application most have constituted another administrative hurdle fraught with uncertainty and delay. In most cases as well there has been substantial corruption associated with the award of tax holidays. This was reportedly one of the main problems with the prior investment code in Tanzania, and a major reason that donors supporting the structural adjustment programs of Tanzania insisted on the removal of discretionary tax holidays in that country.

Business Licenses

In addition to qualifying for incentives and registering a company, there is often a separate business license requirement. In Ghana and Uganda, this is granted by the municipal authorities, and involves payment of a business-licensing fee, which can be an important source of revenues for the local governments. For this reason, they have been relatively efficient at registering businesses.

However, rather than just registering businesses and collecting annual taxes, governments have instated other requirements that make the process more difficult than it need be. In Kampala, for example, the signature of the local government councilman was required on every application. This supposedly was a means of ensuring that there was no conflict with the business opening in the neighborhood, but in practice was a means of eliciting extra payments for the signature. In Tanzania, the required forms were difficult to find and complicated; they are also in Swahili, making it difficult for foreign investors.

Expatriate Work and Residence Permits

For foreign investors, securing a residence or work permit is a mandatory step. This applies also to expatriate employees who may be brought in. Given the stated goal of all the countries in the group to promote employment of nationals, they all exercise controls over the granting of work permits or visas to expatriates. Unfortunately, the way the controls are implemented often interferes unnecessarily and unproductively with FDI. The presumption of most immigration authorities is that such permits are the exception, not a standard aspect of doing business in the country. In some countries, long-standing ethnic tensions in the business community further aggravate the situation. Essentially, immigration departments require (1) that investors demonstrate that they are "serious"—that is, that they are not attempting to use making an investment as a means of securing work papers—and (2) that firms demonstrate that the employees recruited from abroad are essential and have required qualifications that cannot be met locally. In the implementation of these types of controls, however, a number of frustrations for investors inevitably result:

■ *Extensive documentation requirements.* For employees, this typically includes copies of birth certificates, diplomas, testimonies of experience, resumes, employment contract or offer, police records, marriage certificates, medical examination reports, and verification of attempts to recruit locally. For investors, additional information usually includes copies of company statutes or articles, registration verification, promotion center certificates, and sectoral approvals from ministries. Assembling this documentation can take time and be problematic in many cases.

■ *Long delays.* Although delays of a month are standard, the process can take up to six months in Tanzania and up to 10 months in Mozambique.

■ *Corruption.* Bribes for residence or work permits are reportedly common and often are the principal means of expediting the process for foreigners.

■ *Uncertainty.* In Ghana an investor must realize his investment prior to securing a residence permit; until that time he operates on an extension of the initial visa. In others, the standard duration is only two or three years, after which investors and employees face the same process once again. Renewal of employee work permits may be difficult because immigration officers in Uganda, for example, expect that Ugandans should have been trained for these positions during the initial period. Some authorities, such as those in Uganda (the Investment Authority as well as the Immigration Department), rely excessively on academic diplomas as demonstration of qualifications. All of these actions induce an element of uncertainty into the process that can be unsettling for foreign investors in particular.

Two countries, Ghana and Uganda, have begun to recognize that issuance of residence and work permits to foreign investors should be an unobtrusive, easy step in the process of a foreign businessman making an investment. Both countries issue automatic residence and work permits to investors, based on the amount of the investment, with additional work permits available upon the standard application process. However, because this step then requires investors to document the realization of the investment prior to issuing the permits, its value is somewhat diluted.

Securing residence and work permits should be a routine step for foreign investors—making it so is an integral part of promoting foreign investment. However, it can be a particularly difficult hurdle. Few immigration authorities have confidence in the financial realities of hiring expatriates—i.e., that it's much more expensive than hiring nationals—and therefore treat each application assuming the investor is trying to cheat a national out of a job. In addition, because the investors' legal status in the country is at stake, the authorities have enormous leverage over them, and there is usually no way around them—except, of course, to pay bribes. This is one reason why bribery appears to be so commonplace during these transactions.

Tax Registration and Administration

The process of tax registration should be straightforward. Because tax authorities need to know which firms exist in order to collect taxes from their operations, it is to the authorities' advantage to make registration easy. Yet this is not always the case for the following reasons:

■ In Uganda, the Revenue Authority uses separate procedures and identification numbers for registration for corporate taxes and for VAT. Both processes are subject to several sequential steps requiring different forms.

■ Mozambique levies several small taxes, including stamp taxes that apply to all kinds of documents, which can only be secured from the main tax offices. (This applies to materials such as posters for public display, which require individual stamps and seals.)

■ In Namibia, three separate tax identification processes are required. For exempt goods, the Minister of Finance's signature is required, resulting in frequent delays when clearing imports of machinery, for example.

■ Similarly, in Tanzania separate registration processes are required for sales tax, excise tax, and stamp duties, in addition to the registration process required elsewhere in the Revenue Authority for the income tax. Each application requires a physical inspection by a revenue officer.

■ In Ghana, the registration process is, in effect, repeated annually with declarations of projected withholding obligations.

■ In many countries, tax clearance certificates are required for importing or other transactions with the government, as in Ghana and Uganda. This adds another step to already cumbersome procedures, a step that is of dubious value in enforcing tax collections.

Problems in tax registration are a function of the overly complex nature of the tax system in these countries, together with a limited capacity for effective administration. Therefore, in an attempt to impose tight controls, governments have developed arduous and often duplicative registration and reporting requirements. As part of tax reform programs in some African countries, such as Uganda, improvements are being made. However, in these as in other countries, the various reform and collections initiatives may actually render the tax system even more complex, resulting in the major reason small firms avoid registration or any other formalization that would bring them to the attention of the revenue authorities.

Other Licenses and Registrations

Governments may require that most companies apply for a number of other registrations at an initial stage. These include patent, trademark, and copyright registration; documentation of investment inflows with the central bank; and an environmental impact assessment. These requirements tend in nature to be secondary or peripheral to the process of making an investment and vary widely among the countries concerned. They are, however, not without problems, albeit minor ones.

Intellectual property registration varied widely in the countries studied. In some, it was routine and inconsequential, as in Uganda. In Namibia, there was a two-year backlog of patent and trademark applications pending approval or registration. The primary reason was a lack of qualified employees (i.e., typists) to issue the certificates. Trademark registration forms were unavailable in Tanzania, although local bookshops would make unofficial copies. These types of delays and difficulties are perhaps not critical, as many companies do not bother to register trademarks and the like. However, for some businesses, such as manufacturers of branded consumer goods, it may be crucially important. In addition, the lack of effective protection from imitators due to poorly developed registration and enforcement can be a disincentive for such firms to enter markets.

The degree of documentation or registration of actual investment flows is typically a function of the level of exchange controls. In countries with liberal systems, such as Uganda and Ghana, this is accomplished by the commercial banks without the requirement of registration or verification by the central bank; commercial bank documentation of financial transfers is sufficient.[24] In Mozambique, however, the Central Bank must verify inflows of foreign capital in order to facilitate repatriation later. If this is not accomplished, there will be problems upon repatriation of profits/dividends or the original capital.

Environmental assessment of new investment projects is a fast-changing area of screening and regulation. In the days when most countries reviewed and approved all major investments, some form of rudimentary environmental impact was included in the feasibility study. Now, this is often a separate step accomplished by a specialized agency for that purpose. In Uganda, Tanzania and Ghana, environmental management or protection agencies were being established when this research was undertaken. Each was to have the ability to screen all new industrial or commercial projects for environmental impact. However, their procedures were not yet well defined. The general trend was to make an early classification of proposed projects, with the level of review linked to the potential ecological hazards proposed. Thus, a light manufacturing operation with no hazardous materials would not be required to do the full environmental impact assessment that might be required of a factory producing wastes or using hazardous materials. In each country, some form of environmental review was required. For those with discretionary incentives, an environmental review continued to be one of the requirements in the feasibility study.

Conclusion

Cutting through the red tape of registering a company, registering for taxes, getting required approvals, securing work permits for expatriates, and so on should be a series of simple procedures. In most industrial countries, they are simply procedures and formalities that can be completed with a minimum of effort. In the African countries studied, they can be quagmires causing delays and unforeseen costs and always inviting payments to circumvent the law or otherwise solve the problem. Taken together, the entire process can be daunting for new investors, particularly for foreign investors and for smaller domestic businessmen who may have expanded and formalized their operations.

The types of obstacles encountered at this initial stage include the following:

■ Unhelpful, even predatory, bureaucrats unable to provide forms or otherwise facilitate in meeting requirements they are responsible for administering;

■ Delays beyond the time necessary to secure approvals or signatures;

■ Complexities stemming from the need to administer poorly designed incentives schemes;

■ Lack of computerization and lack of capacity in registration or regulatory bodies;

- Multiple, sequential steps required from agencies to process applications;
- Duplication of effort among agencies, which often request the same information;
- Outmoded information requirements that no longer serve any real purpose but that cause needless work for investors;
- Excessive costs stemming from complex requirements in company formation and up-front capital taxes.

As a result, it is common for businesses to need about six months (less in Namibia) to perform the formalities of getting an investment approved, and registering or completing all the other tasks required prior to actually doing anything. These hurdles, however, represent just the beginning. For many businesses, additional specialized approvals are also required. These are examined in the following chapter.

3

Specialized Approvals

M any types of private businesses require special authorization or licensing from various government bodies. In general, this is accomplished on a sectoral or sub-sectoral level, with line ministries[25] or parastatal agencies responsible for initial licensing and regulation. In most countries in Africa, engaging in trade or many services requires no such special license; the types of approvals outlined in the previous chapter comprise the range of initial approvals and registrations required. In some countries this layer of sectoral approval has been eliminated for manufacturing; in others some form of licensing or differential access to incentives has been maintained for industry.

The sectors where entry is restricted, screened, licensed, or otherwise controlled include those that utilize scarce natural resources, depend on use of public property or assets in some fashion, or are simply in sectors that are highly regulated for a variety of reasons related to consumer protection and maintenance of desired market stability. These include fishing, forestry, mining, tourism, financial services, transportation, utilities, broadcasting and media, health services, pharmaceuticals, and so on. Restriction of entry is a key aspect of sectoral regulation in all these fields, as is enforcement of regulations on firms' operations. In many sectors there are secondary restrictions on foreign participation, often in conflict with the language in investment laws requiring equal treatment.

Where there is restriction on entry, there are procedures for getting licensed. In most of the countries studied, the process of obtaining operational licenses tends to be more complex than necessary to meet the goals of sectoral management. There are hundreds of specialized licenses throughout the countries studied. In this chapter, four sectors will be examined as representative examples: industry, fisheries, forestry, and tourism. The administrative procedures and licensing requirements in these sectors represent the broad range of bureaucratic constraints faced by potential investors.

Industry

Investment in manufacturing has been the principal objective of most African countries' investment laws. In fact, whether a firm engages in manufacturing, as opposed to mere trading, is often the definition of "investor" in terms of the law, and in terms of the attitude of governments toward the investor.

Although many countries in Africa and elsewhere have removed industrial licensing requirements as part of their attempts to facilitate investment, many still maintain some form of industrial licensing. In our sample, Ghana and Uganda are the only countries to have opened the field entirely. Table 1 describes industrial licensing requirements in the remaining countries.

The industrial license in Mozambique and Tanzania is a classic example of unnecessary bureaucratic red tape that persists in an otherwise open economy. The role of a special license for industrial projects is a carryover from the preceding policy orientation of promoting industry at any cost with high degrees of protection, incentives, and subsidies. In that policy framework, licensing of new firms was the key step in allocating access to these preferences. In the current liberalized economies that characterize much of Africa today, there is really no role for controlling investment in industry *per se*. The related policy objectives of protecting the en-

Table 1. Licensing of Industrial Investment in Surveyed Countries

Country	Requirements
Mozambique	In Mozambique the traditional licensing requirement for industrial firms involves myriad prerequisites and preparation of 12 separate documents, and can take up to one year to complete. It has been one of the major complaints of the business community, particularly in an era when other countries have abandoned such requirements. To a great degree, it simply adds another layer on other types of approvals, such as those for building design and approval, company registration, incentives approval, etc. with no real rationale for the added scrutiny.
Namibia	A separate fiscal incentive regime exists for manufacturing in Namibia. To qualify, firms must apply for "manufacturing company status." Though technically required only for incentives, the qualification is narrowly limited to industry, so that it constitutes a sectoral rather than general incentive program. It is attractive enough to make it mandatory, for competitive reasons, to pass through the process. Yet there is no clear definition of what constitutes manufacturing, and there is an overlap with other incentives programs, which complicates the qualification of certain firms (i.e., exporters). This additional step typically adds a month to the process of getting initial approvals—up to three months for projects outside Windhoek.
Tanzania	In Tanzania, the Industrial Licensing Board is a mandatory stop for all manufacturing projects with investments over TSh 10 million.[a] The board examines availability of raw materials, economic feasibility, etc., as well as areas assessed by other agencies (environmental impact, utilities demands, etc.). Although this takes three months to complete, projects reportedly are rarely rejected.

a. TSh = Tanzanian shillings.

vironmental, allocating fiscal incentives and so on, are dealt with more effectively by direct policy instruments such as limits on pollution and incentives inherent in the tax code, and do not require a separate screening.

Fortunately, this type of industrial licensing requirement is increasingly the exception, in Africa as elsewhere. The targeting of fiscal incentives to industry is still common, as is practiced in Uganda and Namibia. However, this also is changing as countries increasingly reform investment incentive schemes to eliminate the need for prior screening and approvals.

Fisheries

As a renewable but often over-exploited resource, fisheries world-wide have been subject to controlled access, limits on catches, and regulation of fishing methods in virtually all countries. Although African nations are no exception, ineffective regulation and enforcement have compromised their otherwise sincere attempts to manage this resource. All the countries examined here attempt to license fishing vessels in the waters they control, within up to 200 miles of an exclusive economic zone.[26]

Where the fishing effort is in danger of depleting stocks to the point of extinction, fishing licenses or permits are restricted below demand. In these cases, licenses are typically restricted to favor nationals and those already engaged in fishing, so that new licenses are particularly difficult to secure. In general, the main regulatory tool is licensing of a vessel to fish in territorial waters; there may or may not be a catch limitation on particular species. By controlling the number of vessels, authorities regulate roughly the annual catch.

As a livelihood, fishing has always been important in coastal communities. Many coastal regions host large populations of artisanal fishermen who operate outside of normal licensing procedures, but whose limited technologies act to restrict the impact of their activities on resource levels (except in Uganda, where even artisanal fishing is regulated.) Licensing of commercial vessels, foreign or national, has the additional objective of protecting the interests of these artisanal fisherman, through limiting commercial fishing in their grounds or otherwise ensuring that their livelihoods are not disrupted by commercial-scale fishing.

For these reasons, then, investment in fishing is closely controlled. The legislative regimes that oversee the fisheries sector in many countries are often vague; the lack of transparency in the licensing process contributes to a high degree of corruption. Combined with inadequate resources for effective enforcement throughout territorial waters, the inevitable result is that management of the resource is often ineffective, there is illegal fishing, and governments lose revenues from a potentially lucrative activity. Table 2 describes fisheries licensing requirements in the countries surveyed.

As Table 2 shows, in the countries involved, fisheries licensing is the main tool for resource management. However, because of the lack of enforcement (which requires vessels patrolling territorial waters, except in Uganda), the multitude of restrictions on foreign vessels or firms may be simply ignored. As stocks become depleted, more draconian measures may be called upon. Without effective control of illegal or unlicensed fishing, the range of restrictions on both nationals and foreigners only serves as a further incentive for illegal operations. In the process, a greater degree of control over the resource is lost, including the ability to establish a shore-based processing and export industry, which would benefit from foreign involvement.

Forestry

Forestry as well is a renewable but scarce resource for which effective management is critical to maintaining a productive resource base. For most hardwood forests, once they are cut for timber they are not replanted and do not regenerate quickly to be truly renewable resources. In Africa, forests are on public lands, which are managed by the government. Natural resource ministries or forestry authorities typically use licenses for cutting timber as the main resource management tool. Securing these licenses, however, seldom appears to follow a course suggesting that they be used principally for this purpose. There is a lack of transparency that leads inevitably to long delays, and corruption in the process. Because the regulations governing the forestry sector are often unclear and not well enforced, there is a significant degree of illegal cutting. Not only does such illegal cutting undermine effective resource management and imperil the forests, potential revenues, which could be used for effective management and replanting, are lost. Table 3 summarizes forestry licensing requirements in the countries surveyed.

Table 2. Licensing of Fishing Investment in Surveyed Countries

Country	Requirements
Ghana	In Ghana, fishing licenses are required for commercial fishing, based on a vague application process to the Ministry of Food and Agriculture. Foreign firms or vessels are not allowed, with the exception of offshore tuna fishing, where they must be in joint ventures with nationals. The problem remains that, as in Tanzania, foreign vessels routinely fish in Ghanaian waters unlicensed, landing their catch elsewhere.
Mozambique	Commercial fishing licenses in Mozambique are allocated based on specific type of fishing activity, fishing zone, type of vessel, and fishing technique. Licensing for foreign fishing vessels restricts fishing to open waters beyond 12-mile territorial water limit, and only for tuna. Multiple agencies are involved in issuing licenses for industrial fishing. A new regulatory decree is currently being drafted to monitor fishing; this mandates that every vessel must be inspected before it is issued a license. Because most fisheries activities occur far from Maputo, enforcement is difficult and the fisheries sector in Mozambique is *de facto* largely unregulated.
Namibia	As in Uganda, there is no new issuance of fishing licenses in Namibia. Existing companies that have fishing rights cannot transfer them; as a result, potential new foreign investors must purchase existing companies with fishing rights, undertake joint ventures, or charter the vessels. In spite of the generally solid regulatory framework governing the fishing sector, a few problems remain. There is a lack of transparency in the complex distribution system of quotas. Because fishing rights are non-transferable, banks will not accept them as collateral for loans; moreover, financing in the fishing industry has been characterized by bartering, which is illegal in Namibia.

Unlike the fishing sector, where countries do not have the resources or capacity to patrol territorial waters, illegal timber cutting on public lands is readily enforceable. The persistence of illegal logging requires active complicity on the part of national and local authorities, suggesting that the process is largely circumvented by bribery and corruption. As worldwide stocks of tropical hardwoods have dwindled due to over-cutting, those remaining have become even more valuable. Yet, in the countries noted above, as in others in Africa, (appropriately) restrictive licensing in the name of resource management is not taken seriously, by both the firms involved in

Table 2 *(continued)*

Country	Requirements
Tanzania	Tanzania licenses commercial fishing in coastal and EEZ waters, including foreign vessels. Licenses are issued annually in March, following a stock assessment. Fishing vessels must also be inspected and licensed. Tanzania uses discriminatory fees to limit foreign fishing and encourage local processing. The license fee for a national prawn trawler up to 160 tons would be US$65–84; for an equivalent foreign vessel it would be US$20,000, or US$40,000 if there is no shore-based processing facility in Tanzania. Applications for fishing licenses must be approved by a village authority (if applicable), the district fisheries officer, the regional fisheries officer, and the director of fisheries. Although a 30-day period is stated in the law, delays of up to three months are common—longer if there is uncertainty about the size of the catch to be allowed. In addition, controls on exports of fish from processing plants require health or quality control inspections and licenses for each shipment.
Uganda	In landlocked Uganda there is essentially no commercial-scale fishing and no new licensing of fishing on controlled-access waters such as Lake Victoria. Foreign investors are not permitted to operate on controlled or open access lakes; fishing operations on these waters are restricted to artisanal fishermen. On controlled access lakes, the number of fishing vessels is restricted; existing licenses are essentially handed down. Fish processing in Uganda is also closely controlled and licensed. A Technical Committee of the Fisheries Department is responsible for allocating export quotas to industrial fish processors. These processors have complained that the current quota of 60,000 tons per year is too small and given the apparent excess capacity no new licenses are being issued.

the logging, and those agents charged with enforcing it. A more reasonable approach would be to allow some limited timber cutting, from which substantial revenues could be generated, and use the proceeds for enforcement. Periodic auctions of timber rights are not used in any of the countries studied; rather, there are fixed stumpage or lumber fees, or annual lease/concession payments tied to the area of land. In some countries, such as Tanzania, the system appears to have been designed to maximize opportunities for corruption. This, combined with the financial value of the resources at stake, has engendered a high degree of illegal logging.

Table 3. Licensing of Forestry Investment in Surveyed Countries

Country	Requirements
Ghana	The current policy for granting timber concessions in Ghana is being reviewed. Investors express concern about the lack of transparency; moreover, delays of two to three months are typical. Lumber milling firms are subjected to a government quality control inspection.
Mozambique	Provincial governments grant licenses for commercial logging in areas measuring less than 1,000 hectares. For areas exceeding this limit, licensing must be obtained from the Ministry of Agriculture. Investors have identified a number of problems. Several months are needed to negotiate a concession agreement, partly because of lack of information provided by the government. Investors sign a contract with the licensing authority that must ultimately be published in the *Official Gazette* in order to be valid, causing further delays.
Tanzania	All land, including forestry resources, is the property of the government. Licenses to fell trees in Tanzania are issued for one to three months, whereas in most countries they are issued for two to three years. Tanzanian law does permit lengthier concessions; however, they are generally not issued. The complex royalty and licensing fee structure, coupled with the lack of transparency in the licensing process, creates numerous opportunities for corruption. The extensive illegal cutting that occurs—directly attributable to the cumbersome licensing process—has resulted in extensive losses of potential state revenue; moreover, it has contributed to a high level of environmental degradation. Restrictions on licensing, graduated fees, and a virtual ban on exports of raw logs (except for two species) have done little to rationalize the sector in Tanzania.
Uganda	Cutting timber is open to foreign firms. However, investors have reported delays of two years in obtaining a "License to Fell Trees." The government has admitted that 50 percent of trees in Uganda are being cut illegally. Other administrative aspects of the program also languish: the required deposit for a license—equivalent to 10-15 percent of the value of wood—is supposed to be returned, without interest, after a company completes its activities. However, the Commissioner of Forestry Resources has reported that investors rarely get the deposit refunded. High levels of illegal logging have led finally to a policy of banning all exports of unfinished lumber. However, questionable enforcement of this policy may also simply lead to its circumvention.

Tourism

Tourism is a high-priority development sector for all of the countries studied, one in which both foreign and domestic investment is actively promoted. It earns foreign exchange, is relatively labor intensive, and by definition exploits unique national characteristics. It is also a sector where some form of sectoral regulation is present, including entry screening and operational controls. The reasons for this degree of regulation stem from several issues specific to the sector:

- Consumer protection, in terms of the maintenance of health and safety standards, etc., for patrons of hotels and restaurants;
- The conscious efforts of many governments to develop a defined tourism "product," for which standards must be set and maintained in order to preserve the touristic appeal and image of a country as a destination;
- The frequent desire to limit foreign participation in the sector, as it is seen as one where nationals should be able to have a dominant role; and
- The question of limiting, or optimally pursuing, tourism development and its impact on natural, cultural, and other attractions.

The result is an often-confusing array of incentives and controls that in many cases acts to constrain investment without meeting the policy or strategic objectives that spawned them. Table 4 summarizes procedures for licensing tourism operations in the countries surveyed.

The tourism sector in these countries is underdeveloped both in terms of its potential and in terms of what the countries themselves are trying to promote from a strategic point of view. The policy goal of maintaining standards has prompted all the countries in the sample to micro-regulate many aspects of the business of operating a hotel, restaurant, travel agency, or tour company. There is no doubt that these regulations deter investment that may be at the lower end of the tourist scale, in facilities or operations that do not ostensibly match the standards, and that this is in part their desired effect. However, by limiting entry they also limit competition and ultimately the growth of the sector.

Rather than trying to specify the details of tourism industry firm operations with administrative measures, it may be more productive

Table 4. Licensing of Tourism Investment in Surveyed Countries

Country	Requirements
Ghana	Businesses involved in lodging, food provision, and tour operations must receive permits from the Tourism Board. The board still requires screening and annual licensing of investments in this sector. However, its screening of hotel investments is duplicative of controls administered at other levels by authorities responsible for supervising construction, health, and safety standards.
Mozambique	Tourism is one of many activities licensed by the Ministry of Industry, Trade, and Tourism. The documentary requirements for hotel and tourism licensing are extensive, and include a sealed, verified original copy of all documents in the dossier. A back-and-forth process between the Investment Promotion Center and the Tourism Directorate in the ministry inevitably results in delays and numerous requests for clarification. There is a series of sequential licensing steps once a project is completed that includes multiple inspections, all essentially at the same stage. Prices charged must also be submitted for approval. Result: a long and unpredictable road, each step of which is paved with multiple official copies of notarized, stamped documents and supporting attestations, verifications, and registrations.
Namibia	Tourism sector policies in Namibia are currently being changed. The government is planning to ease tourism development policies and to create a new National Tourism Board that would be financed by a bed-levy tax. Proposed policies would permit local and international companies to develop facilities in national parks (previously limited to nationals.) Until now, however, tourism investment in Namibia has been constrained by excessive and arbitrary regulations. For example, certain entities such as guest farms are required to have at least five bedrooms if located outside municipal areas and at least 10 bedrooms if located inside municipal boundaries. Details are specified down to the size of the mandatory guest mirrors. Hotel projects must be registered (approved) prior to construction, and then are subject to inspections prior to opening, and mandatory grading within six weeks of opening. Hotel

to allow some product differentiation, with easier entry, and a reliance on competitive forces among private firms to act to regulate the market. More foreign participation, particularly among tour operators, would facilitate the maintenance of quality standards, as they would typically be booking tours through affiliates in the tourist-generating countries and would have a more direct interest in having a satisfied clientele. The licensing of hotel managers, requir-

Table 4 *(continued)*

Country	Requirements
Namibia *(continued)*	managers must be licensed as well, and qualifications are reviewed by the Ministry of Environment and Tourism, including a duplication of those reviewed for a general work permit (health and police record).
Tanzania	The tourism sector, historically overshadowed by that of Kenya, has languished due to a number of factors other than obstacles to new investments. However, there are some significant obstacles here: of the 80 to 100 projects approved each year, only 10 proceed to the operational stage. The tax regime for hotels is very high (20 percent of receipts) and contributes to high room rates, which makes Tanzania less price competitive in comparison to Kenya. Travel agents and tour operators are subject to myriad regulations and requirements, including the number of graduates of IATA-approved programs required on the staff, requirements for new vehicles, hotel manager screening and licensing, etc. These types of restrictions simply tend to favor those already in the industry, as they are enforced most closely on entry, when a license is requested.
Uganda	Tour operators, travel agents, and hotel managers are all licensed by the Ministry of Tourism. The guidelines for tour operators and travel agents are overly restrictive, with a number of mandatory requirements at a detailed level. In addition to the licensing of hotels, these types of requirements have acted to curb investment in the sector. However, perhaps the most difficult problem has arisen from the concessions practices in wildlife areas and national parks, the principal tourist destinations. Here the process was discretionary and politicized, with no clear procedures defined. Result: many concessions in potentially valuable national parks sites were granted to groups that simply held them, hoping to sell them at a much higher cost to those with sincere development plans. The lack of development and the demands for more opportunities for legitimate business have led to a reformulation of procedures as well as a focus in the Wildlife Authority on commercial practices and development as an integral part of their natural resources management.

ing demonstration of academic training and suitable experience, is another area where tourist boards appear to feel their own evaluation is required in addition to the investor whose money is at risk and who has recruited the individual in question.

If the expressed purpose of the government is maintenance of a more upscale tourist sector, then there may be other mechanisms, such as higher licensing fees or the auctioning of a fixed number of licenses that would effectively force the industry up-market without the need for complex specifications for each activity in the tourism business. Utilization of grading systems for hotels, tours, and other facilities or products can also be used to promote quality, as many countries have done. Here, detailed guidelines are set for companies to earn quality ratings, not as a legally required pre-condition for entry into the business. In short, there appear to be a number of approaches that would work to achieve these ends more effectively than the sectoral regulation that has persisted in one way or another in all the countries studied. Although some are moving away from this approach, such as Namibia, others appear wedded to the need for a high degree of administrative intervention in the industry.

Conclusion

The main rationale for sectoral licensing is the need to control investment because of some higher concern, such as natural resource management. However, as we have seen, the construction of those licensing systems often acts to make it so difficult that being legal is virtually impossible. Yet the resources are valuable enough, and the will or ability of countries to enforce restrictions so limited, that widespread illegal activity persists in spite of the restrictions. As a result, the sector is thrown into crisis with no resources for the government to deal with the situation, and the institutions responsible are often crippled by corruption and complicity in the illegal activity. In these cases some degree of appropriately limited activity by responsible firms with a stake in the industry could make a real contribution. Yet it is precisely this type of firm that is effectively excluded by the lack of transparency, or opts to invest elsewhere. Finally, in virtually no cases were overtly transparent methods of allocating scarce licenses used, such as tendering by pre-qualified firms, or auctioning of quotas for defined rights in resource exploitation.

In sectors where there is more room for greater economic activity, the penchant of government agencies to overregulate, as in tourism, has also acted to limit needed investment flows. This is not an uncommon pattern in other industries as well. Entry restrictions themselves may be warranted, and certainly are an effective policy tool, but what has not been developed in the same degree are procedures and clear criteria for approval that match the policy objectives driving the regulation. In each country the qualifying requirements are vague and the evaluation criteria undefined, and the result is a predictable mess of corruption and unmet developmental objectives.

It is also at this sectoral level where some remaining overt barriers to foreign investment are to be found. As most countries have liberalized general investment laws to be open to foreign investment, such restrictions have remained or even proliferated when it comes to allocation of scarce resources, maintaining preferences for nationals, and so on, on a sectoral basis. In many cases, this is deleterious to the industry, as in tourism, where foreign contacts and experience are crucial. They also generally contradict the language in investment laws requiring equal treatment, unless cited there as a restricted sector for foreign participation. It is not clear that these restrictions have been maintained for a serious enough purpose to override the assertions of general investment laws that proclaim openness and equal treatment.

In all of these areas there is a rationale for government regulation and control. However, the means of going about this, which rely on extensive administrative requirements for new investors, often fall far short of achieving the original policy objectives for sectoral regulation. This failure makes it difficult to contemplate relaxing any of the existing measures, as the problem is widely perceived as one of insufficient controls and regulation. In each case, however, there are often means by which the original policy goals can be more effectively met, the administrative requirements simplified, and enforcement improved. These often may involve more transparent methods of allocating resource or development rights, such as auctions or tenders, many of which can raise money that can be used to improve agency monitoring and build effective enforcement capacity.

4

Requirements to Gain Access to Land, Site Development, and Utility Connections

Every business must have facilities from which to operate. For many new ventures in Africa, acquiring those facilities—which includes finding and securing land, constructing buildings, and securing utilities services—can be a long and arduous process. Indeed, this set of steps is often responsible for the greatest delays for investors in realizing their projects. Delays may come from inefficiencies in land allocation, uncertain procedures regarding construction of facilities, or lack of capacity in extending basic utilities such as electricity, telephones, and water. Although some businesses, chiefly in the service or retail sectors, may be able to locate existing facilities for lease, most commercial, agricultural, industrial, or similar investments are forced to secure land and develop facilities on their own. The nature of the obstacles posed in these areas for investors varies greatly, from legislative and societal issues in land, to regulatory and institutional issues in construction, to capacity and state ownership/management issues in utilities. In virtually all of these areas there could be dramatic improvements from changes in government policy and administrative practice.

Access to Land

Land tenure in most African countries, including those examined here, is a complex mosaic of historical, cultural, political, and pragmatic influences that make the allocation of land as an economic factor of production anything but straightforward. In most countries, private freehold title to land is quite limited, often prevailing only in those areas that were taken as land for settlers by colonial regimes. Many governments proclaimed all land to be the property of the state soon after independence, yet administration of government land remains bogged down by other factors. Communal systems of land tenure still dominate in many rural areas, where local political leaders exercise important rights of determining use and granting access. These patterns are either tacitly or indirectly endorsed by national or regional political authorities. The traditional rights of "customary tenants" or long-term squatters are often very strong and may defeat formal property rights, or at least complicate their exercise through constraints on the sale or exclusive use of a property. In virtually all countries, freehold ownership by non-nationals is prohibited, or at least requires explicit approval.[27] For all these reasons, there is a very limited "market" in both developed and undeveloped land in most African countries.

One of the most fundamental issues with regard to obtaining access to land in all the countries studied is the tension between traditional, communal uses of land, the authority of local village elders, and the requirements of investors seeking access to land, usually through the national government. National governments may usurp local authority, but the inevitable result is heightened political and social tension. Restrictions on outright foreign ownership are common, particularly for agricultural land. Land access is generally the most politically sensitive issue investors confront in the countries studied. Table 5 summarizes land access requirements in the countries surveyed.

Figure 2 uses the example of Mozambique to show the complexity of property rights and the multiplicity of government agencies involved in obtaining land.

Construction Permits

Once investors have secured land, the next regulatory hurdle is normally getting approvals from various authorities for construction of facilities. The administration of these permits may be at a national or municipal level. Frequently, however, lack of capacity is a serious problem in the institutions responsible for approving plans and inspecting buildings as they are built and completed. The absence of guidelines on building construction standards is a common problem among the countries studied. Modifications to building plans to meet objections raised once construction is underway are common as a result, and can be financially burdensome to investors. In addition, the lack of coordination among agencies involved in issuing building permits contributes to lengthy delays. Table 6 describes the problems investors experience in the construction field overall.

Utilities

The timely provision of reliable utilities services—electricity, telecommunications, water and sewer—is another source of delays, additional costs, and frustrations for investors. Although a few of the utilities in the countries examined are in the process of privatization or otherwise allowing private participation, most now exhibit the following classic symptoms of underperforming parastatal utilities:

- Large backlogs and delays for extension of new service;
- Inability to extend networks, both in population centers where existing capacity is strained and in rural areas where networks do not exist;

Table 5. Land Access in Surveyed Countries

Country	Requirements
Ghana	There are three categories of land in Ghana: state land; traditional land ("stool" or "skin" land); and private and family land. The government's Lands Commission oversees land issues. Nationals may lease land for a period of 99 years; foreigners may lease land for a period of 50 years. For industrial and commercial land, leases for Ghanaians and foreigners are 50 years.
	The commercial real estate market is largely underdeveloped. Because private ownership of land is limited, most investors obtain land from the government. Delays in obtaining land range from three to six months, if there are no special requirements and appropriately zoned land is available. Otherwise, delays of up to two years are common. Inefficient record-keeping, conflicting land claims, and a lack of computerization are the most common sources of these delays. In the Accra region, there is an acute shortage of land available for commercial or industrial use. Although there are plans to develop an export-processing zone near the port of Tema, this will serve only a limited portion of the potential market for industrial/commercial land and facilities.
Mozambique	The Government of Mozambique is revising the legislative framework governing land issues. Under the status quo, land is government property. Under the current law, concessions are granted to foreigners for a period not exceeding 50 years. For small landholders, the new law will facilitate the integration of traditional land holdings. With respect to land classification, the new law delineates the precise use for different types of land: agriculture and forestry; urban development, mining and tourism; and areas designated for special environmental protection.
	With regard to obtaining land in rural areas, the provincial units of the Directorate of Geography and Cadastre lack the technical and staff resources to manage licensing efficiently. A typical result is that more than one title is issued for the same plot of land; moreover, a delay of one to two years in obtaining a title is not unusual. Outdated fee structures complicate the calculation of the cost of rural land. The annual tax payments for land are also difficult to calculate.
	Obtaining land for commercial purposes in Maputo can cost up to US$50,000. Multiple agencies must approve land concessions; delays can last several years. Costs, as stated above, are far in excess of posted price ranges, and confusing information further hampers transparency. Difficulties in obtaining land are compounded by the complexity of property rights and the number of government agencies involved (see Figure 2). One of the few benefits: construction permits are integral to the process and do not require a separate application and approval.
Namibia	In Namibia, the legislative complexities are most clearly reflected in the land classification system. There are five categories of land in Namibia: private urban land; private agricultural land; proclaimed public land available for private purchase; urban land in former

Table 5 *(continued)*

Country	Requirements
Namibia *(continued)*	communal areas; and rural land in former communal areas. Most foreign investors in Namibia obtain private land rather than attempting to secure access to public lands.
	Communal land policy is currently being revised. The existing policy does not permit freehold ownership; landowners operate with "permission to occupy" (PTO) agreements valid for 20 years with five-year renewal options. The laws regulating private agricultural land give the government substantial authority. For example, under the Agricultural (Commercial) Land Reform Bill of 1994, the government (1) is authorized to purchase any agricultural land determined to be "under-utilized" and (2) has the right of first refusal on any land transaction. When the Ministry of Lands purchases a piece of property and the proposed price is unacceptable to the property owner, the Ministry can appeal the case to the Land Tribunal, which can set the purchase price. Foreign investors in Namibia require special permission from the Minister of Lands to obtain agricultural land. An indefinite moratorium on agricultural land purchases by foreigners is currently in effect.
	Obtaining access to land is one of the most problematic issues for investors. The Namibian Government's broad powers with regard to agricultural land access and a scarcity of freehold land discourage local investors from setting up operations. PTO agreements are not recognized as collateral for loans by commercial banks; moreover, there is the following statement on the PTO application: "in the event of compulsory removal of the site as a result of future planning activities, the applicant is responsible for his own removal expenses without any claim against the state." The lack of security posed by the PTO makes commercial banks and investors unwilling to assume financial risks.
	The commercial real estate market for private land in Namibia is fairly well developed in major cities and towns. There is limited availability of industrial zoned land, however, in the Windhoek and Walvis Bay areas. With regard to the land transfer process, there are reported delays of three months.
Tanzania	The legislative framework governing land issues in Tanzania is currently being restructured. Under the existing land policy, created via the Land Ordinance of 1923, all land is the property of the government and can be held only under the following mechanisms: government leases; customary tenure; sub-leases from the private sector. The value of land is determined by the value of the structures on the land, not the land itself.
	Under the proposed new land law, four fundamental provisions will remain unchanged. Land will remain publicly owned and vested to the President on behalf of Tanzanians. Land speculation will be carefully discouraged. Statutory or customary occupancy rights will

(Table continues on the following page.)

Table 5 *(continued)*

Country	Requirements
Tanzania *(continued)*	remain the only recognized forms of land tenure. Obtaining title to land will be determined primarily by occupation and use.
	Delays in obtaining land from the government range from three months to three years and are largely attributable to the unclear definition of the value of land. This, combined with the lack of transparency in the overall process, creates multiple opportunities for corruption. Those with personal connections or a willingness to pay bribes are often best positioned to obtain prime areas.
	There is limited availability of serviced industrial land in the Dar es Salaam area. Most available land in the area is "customary" land, i.e., land that has not been planned. Obtaining access requires complex negotiations with landholders and village chairmen that can last from one to six months. In addition, approval is required from the ruling party, the Chama Cha Mapinduzi, and two courts.
	Delays of six years in obtaining land titles have been noted; a requirement that each Certificate of Occupancy be signed by the Lands Commissioner is a significant factor.
Uganda	The legislative framework governing land tenure in Uganda is currently being restructured. The role of the national government as primary custodian of land is being transferred to nascent district land boards. The Land Reform Decree of 1975—which effectively abolished private ownership of land and created a leasehold system—has been supplanted by the government's decision to restore land to owners who can document ownership through possession of a title. Various laws impose multiple restrictions on foreign ownership. For example, under the Land Transfer Act, the Minister of Lands must approve any land transfer between a non-African and an African who is the registered proprietor of the land in question.[a] Under the Public Lands Act, a government agency cannot lease public land outside an urban area to a non-African.
	Many outdated land laws remain on the books. The Properties and Business Acquisition Decree essentially allows the government to nationalize any property or business at any time. The Rent Restriction

■ Lack of capital to finance expansions;

■ A legacy of years of underinvestment and poor maintenance, hampering the ability of existing networks to service even their limited subscriber base, let alone expand to accommodate new investment;

Table 5 *(continued)*

Country	Requirements
Uganda *(continued)*	Act authorizes rent boards in municipalities throughout the country to set fixed rental rates.[b] In current laws, however, there are also restrictions. The Investment Law of 1991 bars foreign ownership of land for agricultural purposes; this is preserved in the new Investment Act currently under legislative development.
	In Uganda there are different classes of land, with freehold ("Mailo") land available only in the urban areas of the capital region. Large tracts of land in the areas around Kampala have been returned to traditional political leaders, the main one being the Buganda Kingdom. Buganda now acts much like a public sector land authority, with its own land board, which provides long term leases to investors.
	The lack of industrial zoned and serviced land—particularly in the Kampala area, where 65 percent of new investment occurs—remains one of the biggest obstacles to new investment. Complicating this is the fact that complex compensation guidelines for squatters, whose rights are enshrined in the Constitution, have increased delays and costs for investors. Another problem foreign investors encounter is the delay associated with land registration. Although the Ministry of Lands states that a title transfer can occur in two weeks if all relevant paperwork is in order, delays normally range from one to six months.
	The government itself has had difficulties in securing and developing land for an industrial estate. Although the Uganda Investment Authority has been granted three successive plots, there have been problems with each one—including title disputes with former owners, a rush of squatters moving in and constructing houses in anticipation of compensation, and location outside of existing trunk lines for power, water, and sewer services. Result: government efforts have been ongoing for more than three years, with results only now beginning to materialize.

a. This language was aimed at Asians, who may have rights as citizens, but who were explicitly targeted under much legislation governing land, property, and business regulation introduced during the Amin regime.

b. These types of provisions, common in Ugandan laws of the Amin period, are being addressed in a Law Reform program that will update commercial laws.

■ Insufficient rate structures combined with technical and administrative losses that undermine financial performance;

■ Priorities to government over commercial clients, even though the latter pay more reliably than the former;

■ Rate structures that penalize large commercial users;

FIGURE 2
Mozambique: Requirements for Obtaining a Construction Permit and Property Title

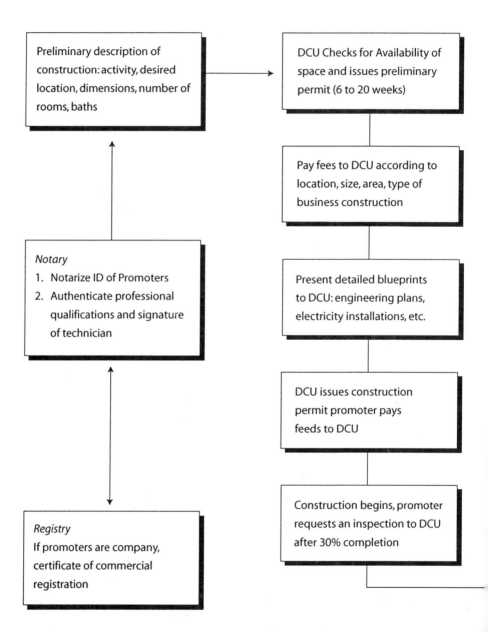

Note: This process takes between six months and two years, and costs US$50,000 for a commercial building.

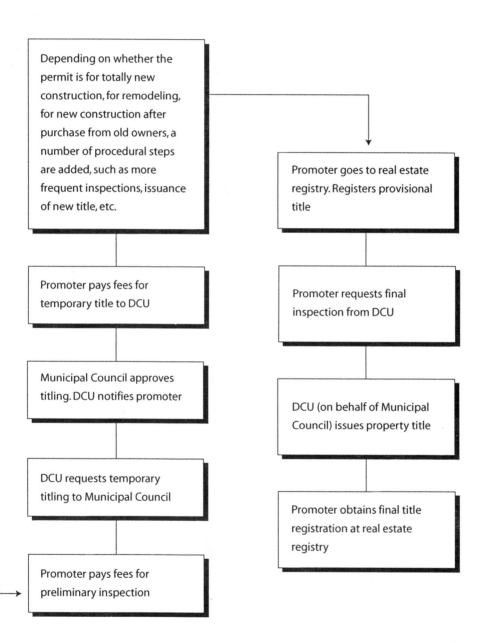

Depending on whether the permit is for totally new construction, for remodeling, for new construction after purchase from old owners, a number of procedural steps are added, such as more frequent inspections, issuance of new title, etc.

Promoter goes to real estate registry. Registers provisional title

Promoter pays fees for temporary title to DCU

Promoter requests final inspection from DCU

Municipal Council approves titling. DCU notifies promoter

DCU (on behalf of Municipal Council) issues property title

DCU requests temporary titling to Municipal Council

Promoter obtains final title registration at real estate registry

Promoter pays fees for preliminary inspection

Table 6. Construction Permits in Surveyed Countries

Country	Requirements
Ghana	In Ghana, three agencies are involved in the development/building permit process: the Town and Country Planning Department, the Lands Commission, and the Engineering and Health Departments of the Accra (or other) Metropolitan Assembly. The overall delay of three to six months in the process is largely the result of poor coordination among these agencies. Because of this lack of communication between agencies, investors are compelled to serve as a "go-between" among them, performing the role of messenger with the plans and application forms. The Town and Country Planning Department consults with the Lands Commission to confirm that a construction site is legally held by an applicant. Although officials from both agencies oversee the process, they recommend that investors personally present the application in order to guarantee its quick review and approval. In a similar fashion, plans and proposals must be circulated by investors to the Engineering and Health Departments. In Accra, and to a greater degree in smaller municipalities, a lack of capacity to review construction proposals hampers the process and further undermines the credibility of the oversight they are providing.
Mozambique	Municipalities in Mozambique manage urban land and grant concessions for building permits. Although buildings on leased land can be transferred, a new title must be issued for the right to use the land. The overall lack of clarity in the law with regard to the issuance of building permits has regularly frustrated investors. Normally permits are issued at the same time as land is titled, but the entire process typically takes from six months to two years.
Namibia	In Namibia, obtaining a building permit is fairly straightforward. Plans are submitted to the chief building inspector for the municipality, who circulates them for review among technical departments as necessary. Permits are typically issued in less than one month in Windhoek, with shorter

■ Cross-subsidization by these large commercial consumers to maintain high-cost service to remote areas;

■ Direct charges to new investors for all of the costs of extension of networks, even if it benefits subsequent users and/or the existing grid network.

Throughout the countries, the electricity installation procedure is generally slow and costly. Routine blackouts, brownouts, and volt-

Table 6 *(continued)*

Country	Requirements
Namibia *(continued)*	times common in Walvis Bay. These are the shortest delays in the countries studied and compare favorably with best practice in general. The most commonly identified problem is the duplicative nature of approvals required from the Namibia Planning Advisory Board (NAMPAB) and the Townships Boards for rezoning, township developments, and other special projects.
Tanzania	In Tanzania, once land has been acquired, investors must obtain a "hoarding" permit that allows fencing to be installed on a construction site. Of the five countries studied, Tanzania is the only one that requires such a permit. A separate permit is issued for the actual construction. This is followed by an inspection program of nine separate points during construction, more than in the other countries studied. These are sequential and frequently incur delays during the middle of construction. As in Uganda, the lack of published guidelines in the form of building codes means that there are a large number of corrections during the course of construction. In Dar es Salaam, the process of approving plans takes about three months; in Mwanza it can take up to a year. These compare unfavorably with delays of less than one month in other countries.
Uganda	In Uganda, construction of buildings and land preparation is overseen by municipal authorities. Town councils must approve all applications for building permits, regardless of the size of the project. The key constraints encountered during this phase are the multiplicity of documentary requirements and the duplicative approval requirements. Indeed, the Town Councils, Factories Inspectorate, and the National Environment Management Authority (NEMA) all essentially review similar, related aspects of each construction project. However, they do so at different points in the process. The absence of effective guidelines on building construction has resulted in a high percentage of corrections required.

age fluctuations damage sensitive machinery. The need to purchase diesel generators to protect against these losses imposes additional costs on firms, especially smaller firms. Generators purchased as backup power sources end up being run for significant periods of time at greater expense. Although businesses are often the best-paying customers for public utility companies, they do not receive priority for installation. Pent-up demand is perhaps greatest in fixed-line telephone service where delays of years are common. Here the

Table 7. Obtaining Utilities in Surveyed Countries

Country	Requirements
Ghana	As is the case in Uganda and Tanzania, slow and costly installation procedures for utilities are the key issues confronted by investors in Ghana. Installation delays range from three to four months for electricity; full installation costs must be paid in advance and businesses do not receive priority for installation. Delays of two months are common for securing water service. A central sewerage system operates in Accra only; septic tanks are used elsewhere. Telephone installation delays of one year are common. Most residential areas in Accra do not have telephone lines.
Mozambique	Power, water, and telecommunications services in Mozambique are also relatively straightforward. Access to new service is not overly problematic. As in other countries, investors must pay the full cost of extension of service. If a company sets up in a location where there are existing networks, installation delays are relatively short. For companies that establish operations in an area without power lines, delays can be longer, a function of the negotiation of the costs to be charged. Due to the ad hoc nature of these assessments, informal payments may be necessary to ensure reasonable services and charges.
Namibia	Namibia stands in contrast to the other countries surveyed here in the provision of utilities. Power, telephone, and water connections can be effected in a matter of days or weeks. Consumers hire private electricians when they want to make new connections. Call completion rates in Namibia are good by international standards: for international direct dialing, the completion rate is 100 percent; for domestic calls, the rate is 98 percent. There are no restrictions on private sector involvement in telecommunications; moreover, international callback services are available. Some of the constraints identified by investors were the limited availability of lines in some areas and the lack of itemized billing statements prepared by Telecom Namibia.
	Because of the chronic water shortages in an arid country such as Namibia, large businesses that require significant amounts of water as a production input will be at a disadvantage. Indeed, national and local authorities are unlikely to approve water-intensive industries, particularly in the Windhoek area.
Tanzania	Electricity installation procedures in Tanzania are slow and costly. Approximately nine steps are involved in obtaining a power connection, and the overall delay is about four months. As in Uganda, the requirement that companies pay 100 percent of installation costs up-front means that the clients are directly financing the incremental expansion of the power grid.
	Although the state-run Tanzania Telecommunications Company Limited (TTCL) has long had a legal monopoly over telephone services in the country, private cellular companies have made significant inroads in recent years. Indeed, private companies such as TriTel and Mobitel offer an alternative with substantially improved service reliability levels. Although TTCL gives priority to installing

Table 7 *(continued)*

Country	Requirements
Tanzania *(continued)*	business phones, a backlog of 50,000 applications exists. Some applicants have been on the waiting list for as long as three years, with 18 to 24 months being typical. Moreover, delay length is inversely proportional to the applicant's willingness to pay bribes; for example, some investors noted that a US$100 payment reduced telephone installation delays to one month.
	Less than 50 percent of Dar es Salaam–based businesses have sewerage connections; most have their own septic tanks. The current bifurcated structure between water and sewerage management has resulted in problems with billing and collection of fees. The proposed reorganization of the Department of Sewerage and Sanitation, which will result in joint billing with the National Urban Water Authority, is intended to correct many of these problems.
Uganda	In Uganda, installation delays for power of up to four months are common. Full payment of installation costs is required up-front, and the equipment reverts immediately to the utility company. The practice of "load shedding," or selective blackouts, has been a fact of life in Kampala for several years due to insufficient generating capacity.
	Businesses do not receive priority for telephone installation, despite the fact that the Uganda Posts and Telecommunications Corporation (UPTC) considers them to be the most reliable customers. The primary problems with regard to telephone installation are the following: low quality of service; lack of a sufficient number of lines; and an archaic billing system. The completion rate of domestic calls in Kampala is only 40 percent during the daytime; in Jinja, only 20 percent of calls are successful on the first try. There is a backlog of approximately 3,000 applications for telephone service in Uganda. Of the 200 to 250 applications received each month, only 100 are serviced. Consequently, delays of one to two years in telephone installation are not uncommon.
	The most problematic water issues are the inconsistent water supply and high water tariffs. In some parts of Kampala, water is supplied only 12 hours per day. Water leakage is estimated at 40 percent of total supply. Billing efficiency (the ratio of water billed to water produced) is generally very low. For instance, the billing efficiency ratio in Kampala is 23 to 40 percent. This figure is partially attributable to the high leakage rate and poor administration of the billing system. The high water tariff is intended to alleviate the impact of these inefficiencies.
	The government initiatives to address these problems include the reform of billing procedures by the Electricity Board to credit firms for purchasing equipment for extension of service; approval of two independent power production projects; commercialization of the telephone company, awarding a second fixed line carrier license; and improvements in the billing, technical and administrative systems of the water company. While there have been some improvements resulting from these measures, little new capacity has come on stream.

excess demand is often absorbed (at greater cost) by cellular service, which in most countries is private. Water and sewer services are chiefly limited to major urban areas and also suffer from delays and backlogs for new service.

Postal Services

Postal services in all the countries studied, as well as throughout Africa, are limited. Because delivery is largely confined to boxes in the local post office, securing a P.O. box is a critical part of establishing a firm, as it defines the official contact point and address. Yet in virtually all the countries studied, there was a lack of available boxes. Firms are required to wait until boxes become available, often for period of months or even years, as is typically the case in Ghana. Some, such as Ghana, have provisions for private mail bags at a higher cost.

Clearly, if delivery to boxes is the only possible option, postal services must install sufficient boxes to meet demand. Although this installation would certainly involve a capital expense, it could easily be recovered through the box rental fees. Although companies have shown their willingness to pay higher fees for this type of critical service, the option is rarely available because private firms are barred from this form of service.

Conclusion

The barriers to investor access to land, site development, and utilities described in this chapter stem from issues that extend beyond red tape and unresponsive bureaucracies. Although there are some administrative and procedural problems in each of these areas, the real source of delays, poor service, and obstructions lies in systemic problems in each of these areas. They are of a fundamental nature, and require long-term efforts to address them.

With respect to access to land, there are important political and social issues involved with leasing or selling public lands to private investors, particularly foreign investors, even though there may be substantial economic benefits for the immediate region as a result. The process will always involve securing formal or informal approvals from a number of different constituencies. Similarly, where approval and monitoring of development plans are concerned, the government plays an important role that should not be minimized. Although it could certainly be better implemented in most of the countries examined, there will be a continued need for screening of plans as well as of inspections and monitoring of actual construction.

For utilities, as noted above, the lack of responsiveness to new service or connection requests from investors is a result of years of poor management and underinvestment by parastatals. Even with privatization or commercialization of operations, there will still be a lag in extending new capacity. And in many countries that have moved to privatize, such as Uganda, the political demands of utility privatization have meant that it often is a long, slow process. Those that have privatized, such as Côte d'Ivoire, are experiencing much greater responsiveness to investors, with delays in connection times measured in days instead of months.

It is surprising that these countries have not yet begun, or are only just beginning, to address these issues by facilitating private development of industrial estates. Doing so would immediately ease the difficulty of acquiring land, which could simply be subleased or sold by the zone developer. The government could act as ultimate landlord, retaining title and offering long-term leases to developers and/or subleases to the final tenants. The developer could also build standard factory shells (for finishing and customization by tenants), or offer build-to-suit services for non-standard requirements. Trunk lines for power, water, sewer, and telecommunications could be brought to the site, with individual connections from there assured by the estate developer, a private contractor, or the utility. These types of fully serviced industrial estates dramatically reduce the time required to establish a new factory building or warehouse for industrial or commercial use. Other types of clustered facilities have catered to service sectors such as informatics, research and development, and small business. They typically are able to offer facilities to customers within 90 days.

These types of facilities in other countries—whether called industrial estates, industrial zones, parks, or export processing zones with a focus on export manufacturing—have overcome just the types of physical and logistical problems encountered by firms in the five countries studied. The barriers described here would be obstacles for the development of the estates but, once addressed on that level, will not confront individual businesses that locate there. In some countries, notably Uganda, Ghana, and Namibia, industrial/commercial estates are being developed, chiefly under the guise of export processing zones. Once completed, these zones should go a long way in overcoming red tape, at least for those firms that qualify. For all the other types of investment, however, there will still be a need to improve the general regimes governing land tenure and use, site development, and provision of utilities.

5

Operational Requirements

Operational red tape comprises the primary regulatory compliance requirements that come into play once a firm has begun, or is about to begin, operations in a country. These are generally a mix of approvals or licenses, registrations related to beginning operations, and regulatory requirements based on sectoral issues. We do not focus here on general issues of business regulation, but rather on those administrative controls likely to be encountered by new investments, and which often serve as barriers or obstacles. The main types of operational requirements can be summarized as follows:

■ *Import/Export Procedures.* Typically, the import/export clearance procedures in all the countries studied are complex and difficult. However, most countries have attempted to streamline customs procedures in recent years. Import and export licenses have been abolished for most goods. In addition, customs tariffs have been revised and the number of discretionary customs exemptions has been reduced. Yet, in spite of these reforms, customs procedures in most countries remain highly non-transparent, with excessive and duplicative documentary requirements.
■ *Foreign Exchange Controls.* Foreign exchange regulations have been liberalized in most countries. In certain cases, however, central

banks continue to be involved in capital transactions; and in some countries the vestiges of exchange controls can be found in out-moded procedural requirements.

■ *Labor and Social Security.* In most countries, procedures for disciplining and firing employees are highly bureaucratic. Mechanisms for resolving labor disputes are generally weak, and most labor laws favor workers. In some cases, registering and complying with social insurance, provident/retirement fund, and other requirements are also unnecessarily complicated.

Some countries have other operating requirements for some firms, such as quality-control product inspections. However, barriers in the aforementioned areas constitute most of the impositions on firms once operations have begun. These are, of course, in addition to tax reporting and payment obligations, which constitute the major source of annoyance to most firms.

Import/Export Procedures

For decades, trade was one of the most closely regulated private business activities in many African countries. This was a result of years of import substitution policies in industry, the maintenance of overvalued exchange rates, extensive exchange control systems, and high taxes on imports and exports, all of which necessitated a bevy of administrative controls on trade. Most of these policies have been abandoned in Africa, including in the countries studied. In some countries, however, remnants of the old institutional and administrative machinery remain.

Trade procedures are also complicated by the fact that African countries derive a disproportionate share of tax revenues from tariffs and other indirect taxes levied on imports. Therefore, tremendous pressure is brought to bear on customs services by both the government, to collect revenues, and from businessmen, to take bribes and allow goods in without paying full duty and tax. This is one reason for the proliferation of duplicative procedures aimed at improving collections by instituting multiple checks and verifications. Yet, as can be seen in Tanzania, for example, this does not mean that corruption and revenue evasion are addressed. Rather, it may simply mean that those who abide by the rules are penalized further by excessive documentation requirements—whereas those who pay bribes are simply obliged to pay in a few more places. Table 8 describes the import/export barriers confronting investors.

Foreign Exchange

As with trade, most countries have liberalized access to foreign exchange, from previous systems of administrative allocation. Now they rely on market-based mechanisms such as auction sales by the central bank or an inter-bank market, with little or no prior authorizations required on current account transactions. In most countries, however, controls exist on capital transactions, and the mechanisms for accessing foreign exchange can be cumbersome. Table 9 outlines the barriers that exist in the countries examined.

The liberalization of foreign exchange controls evidenced in all these countries has significantly improved the operating environment for private firms. With the reliance on market mechanisms, the need for an elaborate array of administrative controls is largely gone. In the countries studied, there are some residual capital controls; however, these mostly require registration of inward investment and some form of documentation or prior approval for repatriation.

Labor and Social Security

Labor regulation is another area where many countries have substantially liberalized during the past few years. Whereas a number of countries formerly required the use of government labor offices to fill positions and exercised veto rights over layoff or firing decisions, most now attempt to enforce basic worker rights rather than dictate contractual matters. Table 10 summarizes the barriers that continue to exist in the labor and social security regimes of the countries examined.

Table 8. Import/Export Procedures in Surveyed Countries

Country	Requirements
Ghana	Ghana has adopted many practices that have improved the performance of its ports and customs services. Examples include the use of three competing pre-shipment inspection companies; provisions for importation "on collection" or before payment of duties for established importers; elimination of the multiple opening and inspection of containers; and operation of Customs and Port services on a 24-hour basis. These changes have resulted in a reduction of the average reported clearance delay from two weeks to three days.[1] Nevertheless, some problems continue to cause delays. The documentary requirements for import clearance—eight separate documents—is excessive. Obtaining necessary forms can be difficult and the Import Declaration form is duplicative of other required forms. Customs is continually under pressure to further reduce the normal clearance time to one day or less, but this is proving difficult to achieve. Reportedly, it has made the improvements so far without any loss of effective performance in revenue collection.
Mozambique	In Mozambique, long-standing problems in customs administration have led to a number of recent reforms. In 1996, the average nominal customs tariff rate was reduced from 18 to 11 percent and the number of discretionary Customs exemptions was sharply curtailed. In an effort to streamline procedures, a British company, Crown Agents, began to manage Mozambican customs operations and recommend revisions in customs legislation; however, a short-term effect of the reform program was a slowdown in clearance procedures as guidelines were strictly followed for the first time. Although these reforms are promising, other procedural requirements still affect trade. Import licenses are still required, and unless the importer is using his own foreign exchange, there are extensive procedural requirements connected with accessing foreign exchange for imports.
Namibia	Namibia is a member of the South African Customs Union (SACU), and therefore does not have the same degree of control over most areas of trade policy as the other countries. Constraints from trade procedures were not encountered to the same degree as in the other countries, although some of the characteristics of SACU, such as relatively high protection via tariff rates and import licenses, may be obstacles for investors.
Tanzania	Even though Tanzania has recently abolished requirements for import and export licenses, customs procedures themselves are among the most complicated in Africa. There are 20 steps and 8 organizations involved in clearing imports, and import clearance delays can exceed 80 days. Importers report having to make an average of 5–10 payoffs per shipment to customs officials in order to accelerate the clearance process.[2] In addition to the delays and payoffs, the following procedures also hamper quick release of imported goods:

Table 8 (continued)

Country	Requirements
Tanzania (continued)	• Although pre-shipment inspection companies inspect goods prior to their shipment to Tanzania, Customs essentially ignores their valuations by re-inspecting goods once they have arrived in Tanzania.
	• Customs refuses to allow pre-shipment inspection companies to issue electronically transmitted Clean Reports of Findings.
	• Customs refuses to accept faxed documents.
	• Customs refuses to accept company checks—all payments are in cash.
	• There are three separate inspections of goods at the port.
	• Importers pay duties before a shipping manifest is lodged. Importers pay duties through commercial banks without knowing whether the ship's manifest has been received by Customs. Customs does not process any paperwork without the manifest.
	• Without a packing list, an entire shipment is manually inspected.
	A Customs modernization program in Tanzania is leading to some improvement. For example, the Customs Department has introduced a Single Bill of Entry, which is intended to reduce minimum delays from seven days to two. However, successfully implementing reforms will require much more than changing forms and procedures; an institutional sea change is called for in this case.
Uganda	Uganda depends crucially on the port services of its neighbors, usually the Kenyan port of Mombasa. Even so, Ugandan Customs repeats many of the obstacles imposed by the transit ports once the goods reach the country for clearance. Delays and circumvention by bribery are common, although not to the degree experienced in Tanzania. The following were some of the constraints identified:
	• Clearance for transit in Mombasa requires SGS (the pre-shipment inspection company) inspection data. Frequently, however, goods arrive in Mombasa prior to the forwarding of the SGS inspection.
	• Goods are subject to arbitrary inspection, delays, and fee charges by Port Authorities and Customs in Kenya. Payment of bribes is commonplace to avoid disruption and delay.
	• There are delays in canceling bonds taken out in Mombasa after goods are cleared in Kampala.
	• A separate bond is required for transit in Uganda. While in theory one bond should suffice under new East African Community agreements, this has not yet been operationalized.
	• Procedures for clearance at the Customs office in Kampala (the "Long Room") are cumbersome, and still require too much time. There is no reason that all the clearance and payment cannot be done in one day, as is often done at the airport in Entebbe.
	• There is only partial computerization of certain steps in the Long Room. No system is yet operational for computerization of the entire process at all clearance points.

(Table continues on the following page.)

Table 8 *(continued)*

Country	Requirements
Uganda *(continued)*	• There is no effective pre-clearance. In theory, this could be done pending final verification with shipping documents and would eliminate any delay for Long Room procedures. In practice, it reduces the time required to two or three days. • The inland terminal facilities at Nakawa operated by TransOcean are poorly designed and ill equipped for the high volume of cargo handled. • The practice of processing of documents in Kampala while holding goods at Nakawa causes additional delays. There are plans to move the Long Room or set up an additional clearance center at Nakawa however these are not yet operational. • There is a high incidence of rejected forms at Nakawa, which Customs and Trans Ocean, the parastatal operator, blames on poorly trained freight forwarders and clearing agents. Yet this is also an indication of either the need for simplified procedures or the degree of (attempted) circumvention that has become the norm. • Payment of duties by bank draft requires an additional three or four days to clear unless the importer's account is with the Uganda Commercial Bank (the bank used by Customs and the Revenue Authority). • Customs performs its own valuations in addition to the SGS verification and may use its own valuation if higher. • Government drawback payments to firms, which are due refunds of duties, have been chronically in arrears and in some cases up to two years. While this has been rectified for the moment, it has been a recurring problem. No other mechanisms exist to relieve duty on exporters' inputs. • Surface delivery takes a long time. The total time requirement for surface delivery of goods from Europe, for example, is 8–10 weeks, of which 4–6 weeks is after arrival in Mombasa, and 10 days to 3 weeks after arrival in Uganda. As in Tanzania, the number of complaints about customs, combined with the need to improve revenue collection, has led to various reform programs. Some, such as the licensing of competing inland container depots, have made a significant difference. Uganda is also one of the few countries to retain trade licensing. An import license, required for all importers, is valid for six months. It is issued by the Ministry of Trade and Industry, presumably for effective monitoring. However, the Ministry does not really control licensing, generates only a small fee income from it, and does not generate any useful data. This is purely a leftover from the days when the Ministry actively controlled trade with import licenses, and is planned to be eliminated.

1. The impetus for these reforms was the original FIAS *Investor Roadmap to Ghana* (1995) analysis, which highlighted the unproductive practices and long delays.

2. This was consistently reported by all the firms involved in trade transactions as principals, customs brokers, agents, or transporters interviewed for the *Investor Roadmap* study. Rather than being the exception, this degree of corruption and delay was the norm.

All the countries studied also have mandatory social security or social insurance programs, with contributions by firms and employees based on salary levels. These were found to require separate registration, reporting of current workers on the payroll, and quarterly or monthly filings. Few problems appeared to arise for firms, however, despite the often inefficient operations of these institutions. Some government bodies required separate payment, rather than pooling of payroll taxes and payment once to the tax authorities. None allowed "opting out" for firms with their own pension plans, or exemptions for expatriate employees. However, this type of flexibility was also not expected by the private sector. If anything, resistance to these obligations appeared to arise from employees, who often reported difficulties in getting payments when eligible. In Uganda, the rate of return used in calculating benefits was routinely less than inflation, so that a worker's accrued pension benefits were often meaningless. Firms generally discounted the public pension programs, considering them just another payroll tax. Larger firms typically have private pension plans for long-standing employees, in recognition of the inadequate public sector benefits. A frequent complaint of workers in smaller firms was that the companies failed to register all employees, and therefore the workers had no benefits.

In sum, although improved labor regulation has given companies some flexibility in making employment decisions, a number of rigidities remain. Only in Ghana were there severe problems that resulted in serious evasion of formal hiring. With social security programs, the types of reforms now being implemented in Latin America to allow for privately run pension programs have yet to take root: poor performance of the public institutions and programs continues to be tolerated.

Conclusion

Regulation affecting business operations has dramatically improved in most African countries over the past decade. Many reforms have been encompassed in structural adjustment or other comprehensive

Table 9. Foreign Exchange Controls in Surveyed Countries

Country	Requirements
Ghana	Ghana has a liberal foreign exchange regime. Although exporting firms are allowed to maintain foreign exchange accounts, they must be approved by the Central Bank, which requires demonstrating a need, projections of export proceeds, and other data. The Bank also reviews requests for foreign loans; however, this is not a consistently applied requirement. Otherwise, most transactions can be effected directly with commercial banks and foreign exchange bureaus, and require neither direct interface with the Central Bank nor prior authorization.
Mozambique	Mozambican laws guarantee foreigners the right to remit loan dividends, profits, loan repayments and invested capital abroad. For amounts in excess of US$5,000, investment registration and repatriation procedures with the Investment Promotion Center and the Central Bank must be followed. Recent regulatory reforms allow 100-percent profit repatriation and full retention of foreign exchange earned in local accounts.
Namibia	In Namibia monetary policy is determined by the country's membership in the Common Monetary Area (CMA), a currency union based on the South African Rand. Under the terms of its CMA membership, four authorized banks administer exchange controls. All exchange control issues in Namibia are referred to these four banks, which in turn direct these issues to the South African Reserve Bank.
	Obtaining an overseas loan requires approval from the Bank of Namibia. Applications are processed through one of the authorized commercial banks. Interest-rate ceilings of two percent over LIBOR have effectively shut out much foreign borrowing, however, given the risk premium required for lending to Namibia. Permission from the Bank of Namibia is also required for residents who wish to open an

programs—in particular, reforms of foreign exchange controls, trade restrictions, and cumbersome labor codes. These reforms have removed many of the rigidities in African business regulation and have aided the closed, highly protected, and static formal business sectors that previously could not attract investment and generate growth.

At the procedural level, however, remnants of the past systems of control often remain as vestigial nuisances for firms. Although the need to fill out comprehensive forms on employment, etc., and submit them to multiple agencies for information only is not by itself a major restriction, it is probably unnecessary and could be elimi-

Table 9 *(continued)*

Country	Requirements
Namibia *(continued)*	overseas bank account. Foreign investors are allowed to apply for Status Investment Certificates, which entitle investors to preferential access to foreign exchange for debt repayment, royalty payment, branch profit and dividend remittances, and repatriation of proceeds from the sale of a business to a Namibian resident.
Tanzania	As in Ghana, foreign exchange controls in Tanzania have been significantly liberalized in recent years. Investors are no longer required to register their investments with the Bank of Tanzania, and the requirement for a Certificate of Registration of Exporters has been abolished. The introduction of foreign exchange bureaus has resulted in the facilitation of conversion and of profit and dividend transfer. Profit repatriation now takes a few weeks; previously, it took several years. The Bank of Tanzania still reviews the terms of overseas loan applications, although the need for this prior authorization is unclear given that its main justification is for statistical purposes, and the Bank rarely rejects any cases. The Bank also does not allow offshore foreign exchange accounts.
Uganda	As in Ghana, in Uganda commercial banks and forex bureaus handle all foreign exchange transactions. The Central Bank issues guidelines and suggested documentary substantiation for transactions, which are administered by the banks and bureaus. A vestige of the former period exists in the Certificate for Externalisation of Funds issued by the Uganda Investment Authority. These certificates were necessary for dividend and profit remittance, as well as some royalty payments, but are technically no longer required. In a somewhat confusing situation, the Authority still issued them when requested, and some banks had asked for them, even though the Bank of Uganda insisted at the time that they were not required.

Note: LIBOR = London interbank offered rate; forex = foreign exchange.

nated with little detrimental effect. Similarly, countries may have liberalized trade, but they still require some form of import licensing—which, though supposedly not restrictive, is again required for informational reasons. The same information can be generated from customs data, but involves a sharing of information and reliance on other's data that is unfortunately still rare in most African countries and not yet evident in the countries surveyed.

It is with customs services, however, that the complex procedures, delays, and corruption are the most pervasive and difficult to address. Here there has been a vicious circle wherein the need to col-

Table 10. Labor and Social Security Procedures in Surveyed Countries

Country	Requirements
Ghana	Unlike in other countries, employers in Ghana are still required to register employment vacancies at one of 56 Public Employment Centers (PEC) throughout the country: the Ghanaian Labor Decree prohibits the employment of individuals who do not have a Registration Certificate Book issued by one of the PECs. Inspectors from the Labor Inspectorate determine whether employees are hired through PECs as opposed to being hired directly by companies. These inspections occur every three to six months.
	PEC operations are generally described as non-transparent. They have helped little to facilitate the placement of workers. Indeed, many investors consider the PECs more of a hindrance than an asset when hiring workers. Result: many businesses hire workers directly, in effect breaking the law to circumvent a highly bureaucratic process.
	Firms operating in Ghana are required to submit quarterly employment forms to the PECs. This is duplicative, given the fact that employers submit employment data to the Social Security and National Insurance Trust.
	The government also requires that all private employment contracts be registered, and that all layoffs be approved by the Ministry of Labor. Both these requirements are unnecessary, and both increase procedural bureaucracy.
Mozambique	In Mozambique, employers are required to submit monthly descriptions of all wages and salaries paid during the previous month. In addition, employers must submit annual holiday charts for their workers along with a copy of the workers' chart during the second quarter of the year. In order to dismiss workers, companies must provide 90 days advance notice; moreover, workers cannot be dismissed without "just cause." Under Mozambican law, *just cause*

lect revenues leads to more checks and controls, which lead to more delays and bribery, and ultimately to questionable increases in revenues. Without wholesale institutional reform, improvements can be difficult to achieve. Mozambique took the drastic step of essentially contracting out its customs service to a foreign company. Other

Table 10 *(continued)*

Country	Requirements
Mozambique *(continued)*	means nothing less than an offense against the law or a breach of the worker's employment contract, so that it is difficult to lay off employees for economic reasons.
Namibia	In Namibia, only the overly complex procedures required to lay off workers appeared to pose problems for investors. This, combined with high severance pay requirements, constitute a severe rigidity in the labor regime.
Tanzania	Labor–management relations in Tanzania are generally poor. There is only one legal labor union plus twelve industrial unions with no legal status. Investors encounter a weak dispute resolution mechanism. Labor laws and the Conciliation Board severely restrict an employer's ability to dismiss workers. Indeed, the law compels employers to hire workers on a temporary basis. Tanzania's Industrial Court has also been identified as a barrier to investors: final decisions in Industrial Court cases can take up to five years, and many decisions have resulted in company bankruptcies.

Although the Tanzanian wage structure is low, workers enjoy generous statutory fringe benefits. Tanzania's fringe benefit ratio of 45 percent compares unfavorably with the 25–35 percent average in many developing nations. |
| Uganda | In contrast to Ghana, there are no labor-oriented licensing requirements with the Ministry of Labor and Social Affairs in Uganda. In general, foreign investors have not encountered problems with Ugandan labor laws and regulations. Factory inspections, which are supposed to be conducted annually, are rarely accomplished because of a lack of resources at the Factories Inspectorate. |

countries have preferred more-incremental approaches that so far have yielded quite minimal results, with the possible exception of Ghana. Until customs administration can be improved, the cycle of complex procedures, evasion and bribery will continue to undermine trade in the region.

6

Conclusions

As a result of the administrative red tape described briefly in this paper, establishing a new firm in Africa can take a long time, requires persistence, and often means additional expenses whose nature and size are difficult to predict. In Ghana and Uganda it can take one or two years to establish a business and become operational; in Tanzania and Mozambique, 18 months to three years; and in Namibia, six months to a year. By contrast, doing so in Malaysia might take six months.[28]

Origins of Excessive Red Tape

The types of problems encountered can be grouped according to origins and characteristics, as follows:

■ Poor policy formulation, wherein the laws cannot achieve their ostensible goals because excessively complicated and difficult administrative procedures are needed in order to implement them properly (e.g., investment screening for tax holidays in Mozambique and Uganda, industrial licensing in Tanzania and Mozambique, and outmoded labor laws in Ghana);

■ Reasonable policies, but problems persisting with institutions and procedures that have not been reformed (e.g., trade licenses in

Uganda and Mozambique and multiple registration and reporting requirements for tax authorities in all countries);

■ Complex procedures for reasons of control, revenue collection, and the like (e.g., customs procedures in Uganda and Tanzania, company registration in Mozambique, and expatriate work permits in Tanzania); and

■ Lack of capacity to implement regulations (e.g., registrars general in Ghana, Tanzania, and Uganda; trademark registration in Namibia; and sectoral licensing in natural resource exploitation, such as fisheries and timber, in all the countries surveyed).

Recommendations

Reducing or eliminating the red tape in a comprehensive manner can be quite difficult. The nature and origins of the problems are often different, and vary among countries. The sheer multitude of small constraints, and hence of remedial measures, makes it difficult to tie them together in some form of package. After all, the constraints are related only in the minds of potential or actual investors who must plow through them. Moreover, they are typically too detailed for the attention of major reform programs, such as are undertaken as part of structural adjustment or other policy reform operations supported by donors. Indeed, all of these constraints have survived such reform programs. Institutionally speaking, a range of cross-cutting issues invades the turf of a host of governmental agencies, each of which has its own mandate. Nevertheless, some approaches have so far proven useful in implementing the reforms identified in these types of analyses.

Presenting the Big Picture

Giving all the organizations involved the "big picture" of what it takes to start a business—from the investor's perspective—has increased awareness of the reality facing private investors, as well as the level of duplication required by various agencies. On completion of each of the studies on which this paper is based, a workshop lasting two days was convened to bring the various agencies together and provide a forum for their reaction to the criticisms of their practices, and for direct dialogue with the private sector. Dissemination of the analytical results generated interest among the business community, providing some rigorous support for what have often been perceived by them as unsubstantiated complaints. Many participants on the government side confessed they had no appreciation for how difficult the entire process was; they only knew their small piece of it. These workshops led to a number of immediate actions taken, often at the procedural level, based on the discussions in the workshop. These typically involved streamlining procedures or eliminating steps that are duplicated among agencies.

High-level Political Support

Finding one or more key persons or organizations in both the government and the private sector to press for implementation of reform is essential. In Ghana, this was done through the Gateway Secretariat, a public-private sector group formed to identify and press for measures to make concrete improvements in the investment climate. In Namibia and Uganda, the investment promotion agencies themselves were the primary champions and provided the continuity required to keep these otherwise secondary reform measures in focus. In Tanzania, strong press interest and coverage, and key individual backers in the government and private sector have kept up pressure for reforms and implementation. In Mozambique, a key minister has devoted substantial effort to pressing his colleagues for action on the many areas of improvement needed.

Pilot Implementation Efforts

Where procedural changes and capacity building are the primary response to the problems identified, pilot projects can be effective. These efforts can work with a limited number of agencies that are willing to experiment with reform and engage in fundamental change, and which participate in pilot projects on a self-selecting basis. Supporting this interest—with additional inputs of technical expertise; assistance in redefining procedures, information requirements, and approval processes; and, in some cases, financial and technical resources—has also been productive, and gives the participating agencies some reason to undergo reform. Although proceeding with reforms may reduce their bureaucratic power from a control perspective, their prestige may increase within a reform-minded government.

These agencies can then serve as models for some of the more recalcitrant ones. In Namibia, for example, the municipal government in Windhoek engaged in a "reinvention" exercise that resulted in (1) setting up a customer service window for businesses and (2) focusing staff training on how to deal with investors and private companies with licensing or registration obligations. In Uganda, a USAID private sector project has worked with the Registrar General's office to computerize operations and support a change in procedures that will make the office financially self-sufficient. In Tanzania, the Immigration Department, following an in-depth review assisted by outside experts, is reducing the average time of issuing work permits from six months to two weeks. In Ghana, the Customs and Port authorities worked together to reduce the typical clearance time for imports from two weeks to three days; they are continuing efforts to reduce it further.

Attitudinal Change

These are isolated successes in a complex field where other problems persist. Nevertheless, they have proved to be important examples for other agencies where there is resistance to reform. All efforts were developed with the active participation and involvement of technically competent line managers and operational staff in each organization. Although they may have been inspired by higher level political support and pressure, ultimately the reforms' success depended on those staff and managers being fully on-board throughout the process, rather than receiving dictation from an outside body.

In order truly to change the climate for investment, those in government must believe that at least part of their job consists of service provision to the private sector, and they must take that role seriously. This often requires a major change in perspective, and takes considerable effort to inculcate among the various bureaucracies. Instilling this kind of "customer-service mentality" into organizations previously oriented toward exercising control and enforcement over private firms is a difficult task. It has been one of the fundamental tenets of the "reinventing government" movement in the United States and other industrial countries, where it has achieved some success, often on a local level. In developing countries it is gradually entering the lexicon of good governance, as countries focus more on the delivery of public services by their government agencies. Those countries that do make some significant strides towards changing the attitudes and perspectives of officials dealing with private businesses will be the ones that, in the end, can overcome the stigma associated with doing business in Africa—i.e., that bad governance in one form or another will always be present—and attract investor interest.

Deeper Policy Reforms

On the policy front, government officials must believe that these types of reforms—to extend liberalization and facilitate private investment—are in the best interests of the country. In a number of cases the policies and their administrative requirements are simply no longer appropriate and should be eliminated. Yet there may be substantial bureaucratic self-interest in perpetuating them, or there may be strong interest groups benefiting from them in the private sector. Placing these difficult reforms in the context of explicit documentation of the complexity of the investment environment has helped broaden support for change. In Uganda, presenting the study results helped galvanize a consensus to simplify the investment code and eliminate tax holidays.

Emphasis on Stakeholder Input

These reforms will ultimately fail if they are viewed simply as requirements from the World Bank and IMF and are not supported both by the government and by those elements of civil society affected negatively in the short run. When this has happened, the implementation has always fallen short, with second-tier obstacles remaining in place or measures being enacted that are counter to the spirit, if not the letter, of the reforms. The Bank is consciously engaging in efforts to broaden the stakeholder base consulted, both when developing country assistance strategies and when building public consensus on policy reform initiatives it may be supporting.

Conclusion

Each of the countries discussed in this report has made significant progress since the original analyses brought these issues to light. In that sense, the situation is already better than that portrayed in this summary presentation. However, certain difficult, even intractable obstacles, such as those preventing access to land, persist to this day. Some agencies are simply unwilling to give up the degree of control and discretion they currently exercise, and the political will to override them does not exist.

In other African countries, and in other regions as well, there are a host of problems similar to those encountered in Ghana, Namibia, Mozambique, Uganda, and Tanzania. Those countries too can benefit from a detailed assessment, from an investor's perspective, of what is needed to set up a company; obtain all the necessary approvals, licenses, and registrations; find a site and open a facility; and begin operations. Addressing these administrative barriers to investment is entirely within the powers of African governments, and can make a real contribution to improving the investment climate, attracting more domestic and foreign private investment, and ultimately creating sustained economic growth.

Notes

1. Foreign Investment Advisory Service, *The Investor Roadmap to Ghana* (1995), *Administrative Constraints to Investment in Namibia* (1996), *Mozambique: Administrative Constraints to Investment* (1996), and *Uganda: Administrative Constraints to Investment* (1997); and The Services Group, *The Investors' Roadmap to Tanzania* (unpublished report for USAID, 1997).

2. Mining is perhaps the most important of resource-based sectors in Africa. Due to its particular characteristics, the sector was not addressed directly in this research.

3. Foreign Investment Advisory Service, *The Investor Roadmap to Ghana* (1995), *Administrative Constraints to Investment in Namibia* (1996), *Mozambique: Administrative Constraints to Investment* (1996), and *Uganda: Administrative Constraints to Investment* (1997); and The Services Group, *The Investors' Roadmap to Tanzania* (unpublished report for USAID, 1997). These papers and consultants reports done for client governments are not usually available to the public.

4. See, for example, Lawrence Bouton, Christine Jones, and Miguel Kiguel, *Macroeconomic Reform and Growth in Africa: Adjustment in Africa Revisited* (Washington, D.C.: World Bank Policy Research Working Paper, 1994).

5. See, for example, Zéphirin Dabré, "The Challenge of Implementing Reform in Sub-Saharan Africa," in World Economic Forum and Harvard

Institute for International Development, *The Africa Competitiveness Report: 1998* (Geneva: World Economic Forum, 1998).

6. This perspective forms an integral part of the World Bank's Structural Adjustment Policy Review Initiative, a dialogue with NGOs and other critics of Bank adjustment programs, represented by the Development Group for Alternative Policies. For a summary, see "BankCheck: SAPRI" in *BankCheck Quarterly*, April 1997.

7. UNCTAD, *World Investment Report 1997*, p. 56.

8. *Adjustment Lending in Sub-Saharan Africa: an Update*, World Bank Operations Evaluation Study, 1997.

9. This measurement is not strictly comparable across countries. However, in general, in other developing countries investment agencies report implementation rates of 30–50 percent, or even higher. Most countries that attract large amounts of FDI, with the notable exception of China, do not have licensing requirements except in certain sectors, so the question of an implementation rate does not arise.

10. *Aide-Memoire sur le soutien à court terme de l'investissement en Côte d'Ivoire*. FIAS report, January 1993.

11. Subsequent work has been undertaken by FIAS in Mali, Swaziland, Lesotho, Madagascar, Mauritania, Jordan, Bolivia, Latvia, and Senegal; and by The Services Group in South Africa, Malawi, Zambia, Kenya, Morocco, and the Dominican Republic. The Services Group has been primary consultant to FIAS in these administrative barriers studies and is undertaking a benchmark analysis of Chile, Hungary, Mauritius, Malaysia, and Dubai. Most of the projects were co-financed by USAID, which has been an early and consistent supporter of this effort. Other financial support has come from UNDP and IFC trust funds.

12. Hernando de Soto, *The Other Path: the Invisible Revolution in the Third World* (New York: Harper & Row, 1989).

13. Tyler Biggs and Pradep Srivastava, *Structural Aspects of Manufacturing in Sub-Saharan Africa: Findings from a Seven Country Enterprise Survey* (Washington: World Bank Discussion Paper No. 346, 1996).

14. A. Brunetti, G. Kisumko, and B. Weder, *Institutional Obstacles to Doing Business* (World Bank Policy Research Paper, 1997) and *How Businesses See Government* (IFC Discussion Paper No. 33, 1997).

15. Brunetti and Weder, *Investment and Institutional Uncertainty: A Comparative Study of Different Uncertainty Measures,* International Finance Corporation Technical Paper No. 4, 1997.

16. D. Stryker, N. Beltchika and M. Thiam, "Les coûts de transactions au Cameroon," Draft Report prepared by Associated for International Resources and Development for the World Bank, 1997.

17. Albert Gore, *From Red Tape To Results: Creating A Government That Works Better & Costs Less: Report Of The National Performance Review* (Washington, D.C.: U.S. G.P.O., 1993). See also Donald F.Kettl, *Reinventing Government?: Appraising the National Performance Review* (Washington, D.C.: Brookings Institution, 1994).

18. David Osborne and Ted Gaebler, *Reinventing Government: How the Entrepreneurial Spirit is Transforming the Public Sector* (Reading, Massachusetts: Plume Books, 1992).

19. This is *not* a function of the difference in legal systems between common and civil law countries and their company laws or commercial codes. In Mali, for example, registration of a company is normally done in two days, even though it, too, involves multiple steps.

20. In Uganda, a circular tangle of red tape requires that a foreigner register his company prior to getting a residence permit, whereas the Companies Act requires resident foreign shareholders to demonstrate they have a residence permit as part of the application for registering a company. The registrar and the Immigration Department, to their credit, are pragmatic about processing these applications.

21. Ibrahim Shihata, "Recent Trends Relating to Entry of Foreign Direct Investment," *ICSID Review: Foreign Investment Law Journal,* Vol. IX, No. 1 (Spring 1994).

22. However, in a provision little noticed at the time of the reform, the Tanzania Investment Centre maintained its ability to approve firms for duty exemptions, even though they are otherwise now handled "automatically" by Customs. This is another example of a reform undermined by procedures and bureaucratic self-interest.

23. The Investment Code, 1991. Uganda, following the lead of many other countries, is revising its Investment Code and incentive system to eliminate tax holidays and approval-based incentives.

24. There is a separate step required to document minimum investment levels; this is accomplished with the investment promotion agencies, as noted earlier in this chapter.

25. Ministries dedicated to specific subsectors.

26. Lake Victoria and other inland bodies are the only waters controlled by Uganda.

27. This prohibition is not typically found in francophone Africa, where foreign individuals or companies may secure a *titre foncier* that is the equivalent of freehold title.

28. These estimates do not include the time required for construction of facilities.

References

Biggs, Tyler, and Pradep Srivastava. *Structural Aspects of Manufacturing in Sub-Saharan Africa: Findings from a Seven-Country Enterprise Survey.* World Bank Discussion Paper No. 346. Washington: World Bank, 1996.

Bouton, Lawrence, Christine Jones, and Miguel Kiguel. *Macroeconomic Reform and Growth in Africa: Adjustment in Africa Revisited.* Policy Research Working Paper. Washington: World Bank, 1994.

Brunetti, A., G. Kisumko, and B. Weder. *Institutional Obstacles to Doing Business.* Washington: World Bank Policy Research Paper, 1997.

———. *How Businesses See Government.* International Finance Corporation Discussion Paper No. 33. Washington: IFC, 1997.

Brunetti, A., and B. Weder. *Investment and Institutional Uncertainty: A Comparative Study of Different Uncertainty Measures.* IFC Technical Paper No. 4. Washington: IFC, 1997.

Dabré, Zéphirin. "The Challenge of Implementing Reform in Sub-Saharan Africa." In World Economic Forum and Harvard Institute for International Development, *The Africa Competitiveness Report: 1998.* Geneva: World Economic Forum, 1998.

Development Group for Alternative Policies. "BankCheck: SAPRI." *BankCheck Quarterly,* April 1997.

Foreign Investment Advisory Service. *The Investor Roadmap to Ghana.* Washington: FIAS, 1995.

————. *Administrative Constraints to Investment in Namibia.* Washington: FIAS, 1996.

————. *Mozambique: Administrative Constraints to Investment.* Washington: FIAS, 1996.

————. *Uganda: Administrative Constraints to Investment.* Washington: FIAS, 1997.

————. *Aide-Memoire sur le soutien à court terme de l'investissement en Côte d'Ivoire.* Washington: FIAS, January 1993.

Gore, Albert. *From Red Tape To Results: Creating a Government That Works Better and Costs Less: Report of the National Performance Review.* Washington: U.S. G.P.O., 1993.

Kettl, Donald F. *Reinventing Government? Appraising the National Performance Review.* Washington: Brookings Institution, 1994.

Osborne, David, and Ted Gaebler. *Reinventing Government: How the Entrepreneurial Spirit is Transforming the Public Sector.* Reading, Massachusetts: Plume Books, 1992.

The Services Group. *The Investors' Roadmap to Tanzania.* Unpublished report to USAID, 1997.

Shihata, Ibrahim. "Recent Trends Relating to Entry of Foreign Direct Investment." *ICSID Review: Foreign Investment Law Journal,* Vol. IX, No. 1 (spring 1994).

de Soto, Hernando. *The Other Path: the Invisible Revolution in the Third World.* New York : Harper & Row, 1989.

Stryker, D., N. Beltchika, and M. Thiam. "Les coûts de transactions au Cameroon." Draft report prepared by Associates for International Resources and Development for the World Bank, 1997.

UNCTAD. *World Investment Report 1997.* Geneva: United Nations, 1997.

World Economic Forum and Harvard Institute for International Development. *The Africa Competitiveness Report, 1998.* Geneva: World Economic Forum, 1998.

World Bank. *Adjustment Lending in Sub-Saharan Africa: an Update.* Washington: World Bank Operations Evaluation Study, 1997.

Cutting Red Tape:
Lessons from a Case-based Approach to Improving the Investment Climate in Mozambique

Louis T. Wells, Jr.
Timothy S. Buehrer

Acknowledgment

Louis T. Wells is the Herbert F. Johnson Professor of International Management at the Graduate School of Business Administration, Harvard University. Timothy S. Buehrer is a Project Associate at Harvard Institute for International Development (HIID). At the time this research was conducted, he was HIID Chief of Party in Mozambique. The authors express their thanks to the Foreign Investment Advisory Service, the Harvard Institute for International Development, and the Harvard Business School for providing support for this research. And they are especially grateful to the company managers and many government officials who were generous in spending their time relating the story of Mozal to us. The authors would like to acknowledge the helpful comments on earlier versions of this paper from Rafael diTella, Benjamin Esty, Robert Kennedy, Debora Spar, and Dale Weigel.

Executive Summary

In the mid-1990s, Mozambique recognized that its new policies to attract more foreign investment were being frustrated by the red tape that plagued anyone doing business in the country and which damaged the country's image abroad. In 1995 the Mozambican government began a program to reduce bureaucratic barriers to investment. The program eventually comprised four steps:

1. A series of annual private sector conferences to create awareness in the government of the problems faced by business, to build pressure for reform, and to provide a forum for progress checks;

2. The preparation by FIAS of a detailed catalog of bureaucratic procedures required of business, so that targets for reform could be specifically identified;

3. The creation of an Inter-ministerial Working Group to Remove Administrative Barriers to Investment, with the goal of bringing minister-level pressures to bear on reform; and

4. A case-based approach to build experience based on one important investment project.

This study focuses on the last of these steps, the case-based approach. The study describes how the approach worked, what it accomplished, and what actions are required to replicate it elsewhere.

The idea of the case-based approach was to select an important proposed investment that had high-level backing, and then to create a special structure that would engage company managers and government officials to work together to solve actual problems, as those problems were being encountered by the investor. The case selected was that of Mozal, a proposed $1.3 billion aluminum smelter.

A two-tier negotiating structure was designed to move the negotiations quickly toward the necessary agreements. The first tier comprised ministers, whose backing and eventual approval was required for the project, but who did not have the time to conduct detailed negotiations. The second tier was made up of high-level representatives from ministries, who were to negotiate the actual basic investment agreement.

For the implementation stage, a third tier was added to the structure, to involve technical people from the company and bureaucrats who were at a level in government where implementation problems arose. In the process, government representatives on the second and third tiers developed expertise on the project and, more important, on bureaucratic problems businesses faced. Moreover, there emerged a network of officials who could solve bureaucratic problems for future investors and who could continue to press for reform in the future. The expertise and the network were both important in the successes of the experiment.

The case-based approach can be credited with a number of accomplishments in Mozambique:

1. This set of negotiations led to the relative rapid completion of a basic agreement and the subsidiary agreements needed for this project;

2. The structure created for the Mozal negotiations established a model that promised to move along negotiations for other large projects;

3. The joint problem-solving effort resulted in the elimination of a number of bureaucratic barriers and the solutions worked out for this case established precedents that future investors could use to deal with some remaining barriers;

4. The experience created a corps of officials in various ministries and in the investment promotion agency who could help future investors deal with bureaucratic problems; and

5. The case-based approach increased the detailed knowledge, the status, and networks of a group of officials who became champions of continuing reform of the bureaucracy.

By 1999, there was evidence that the four steps to attacking red tape were improving the reputation of Mozambique among foreign investors.

A carefully structured case-based approach is, the study argues, a potentially important complement to other steps to reduce bureaucratic barriers to investment. The study reports in detail how the special structure was built and operated. The study concludes that certain steps must be taken, if such a structure is to work. The report explains nine government actions that should enable another country to succeed with a similar approach in a program to attack red tape: build commitment on the part of officials to reform, select one important and appropriate investment project, discourage direct negotiation at the top of government, build a multi-tiered structure, provide high-level government officials at the second tier, allow flexible representation, formalize procedures in certain ways, extend the process into the implementation stage, and institutionalize the structures and capture the learning from the experience.

1

Introduction

T his is a success story, with important lessons for other countries that are trying to attract foreign investment. In it, the government of Mozambique, one of the world's poorest countries, works with managers from a multinational minerals company to improve the country's investment climate. The approaches created to speed the negotiation and implementation of a huge aluminum smelter project, Mozal, provided a number of benefits. First, unlike other large projects proposed in Mozambique, this investment moved through the negotiation and implementation stages with considerable dispatch. Second, the case provided a model approach for negotiating other very large projects. Third, solutions were found in the process for reducing a number of bureaucratic barriers, benefiting this and subsequent investors. Fourth, experience in working on this case created a cadre of knowledgeable and influential government officials to whom subsequent investors could turn for help in dealing with red tape. Fifth, and perhaps most important, these officials became champions of simplifying bureaucratic procedures in Mozambique.

In the mid-1990s, Mozambique was recovering from nearly two decades of civil war. Moreover, it had been attempting for almost ten years to throw off the vestiges of its earlier centrally planned economy.[1] As part of its new development program, Mozambique sought foreign investment. Mozambique's experience, however, was like that of many other developing countries: new policies were announced at the top of government, but where implementation required changes deep in the bureaucracy, the new policies had much less effect than anticipated. Multinational firms continued to show little interest in the country.

In spite of widely heralded reforms and economic progress, Mozambique still ranked 18th out of 23 African countries in the 1998 competitiveness index calculated by the World Economic Forum.[2] Business people's ratings of burdens of government regulations, precision of regulations, state interference, and time required to obtain permits placed Mozambique among the last three of the 20 African countries ranked on these factors.[3] One business-oriented report said that starting a new enterprise still required 12 procedures, 151 steps, and 70 government organizations, and that conducting the process sequentially could take as much as five years.[4] Reforms had created macro-economic stability and even liberalized many laws, but they had not reached far into the bureaucracy, where many regulations, procedures, and attitudes from the period of central planning persisted.

By 1995, high-level officials in Mozambique were well aware that the plethora of regulations, number of required permits, and attitudes of mid- and lower-level officials posed barriers to the foreign investment that the country wanted. So far, much of the foreign investment that had come to Mozambique had been from companies that had been in the country before independence. Many investments were purchases of assets that had become state property in past nationalizations. New large projects, especially involving investors without experience in the country, were proving very hard to attract.

Initial Steps

Concerns about red tape led Mozambique's government to take four steps in a program that can be emulated elsewhere. The *first step* was a series of annual "Private Sector Conferences,"[5] which served to identify the importance of red tape as a barrier to investment and to press government officials for action.[6] The *second step* was the preparation of a detailed catalog of such barriers. Since officials lacked specific information about exactly where problems lay, the Foreign Investment Advisory Service (FIAS)[7] was invited to prepare a report for the 1996 "Second Private Sector Conference."[8] The final FIAS report (November 1996) listed—and in most cases diagrammed—the steps that investors had to go through.[9] It suggested which procedures could be eliminated, based on experience elsewhere, and it proposed changes that would make it easier for investors to navigate the steps that ought to remain. Thus, the final report provided a guide and benchmarks for progress in eliminating unnecessary red tape. The *third step*, a result of the discussions in the Conferences, was the creation of a high-level government team to lead the attack on red tape, the Inter-ministerial Working Group to Remove Administrative Barriers to Investment, which would report to the Council of Ministers. This team, chaired by the Minister of Industry, Commerce, and Tourism, with the Minister of Planning and Finance as Vice Chairman, included all the economic ministers. This Working Group invited FIAS to return to Mozambique to work out a careful plan of action.[10] The Group reported progress on the resulting plan at subsequent annual Private Sector Conferences.

These initial steps led to some early progress in reducing red tape, as reported to the Third and Fourth Private Sector Conferences.[11] Most of the progress was on problems embodied in legislation or explicit regulations. Especially important, for example, was the reduction in the high cost of registering or incorporating an entity in Mozambique. The FIAS study reported that costs of company registration could exceed 10% of a company's initial capital, with 6% or 7% being common. In response to the criticism of these costs, government acted to reduce them by some 90%.[12]

Interestingly, some of the negative effects of red tape were reduced without changing the underlying legislation, regulations, or formal procedures. Foreign exchange regulations, for example, remained largely intact and bureaucratic procedures for a foreign firm remitting earnings survived. Yet, in practice, most foreign exchange transactions became free. Paperwork still had to be completed and stamps obtained, but applications for foreign exchange were routinely approved. Similarly, much paper work remained for foreign firms that applied to make small investments in Mozambique. Rather lengthy applications had to be submitted to the Investment Promotion Center (Centro de Promoção de Investimentos, or CPI), forms that were designed for the days when the government supposedly carefully screened and evaluated proposals for foreign investment for their economic and social impact. Yet, the evaluation of proposals was largely dropped and approvals for small investments were generally quickly forthcoming.

Although the conferences, the red-tape study, and the Inter-ministerial Working Group led to the reduction of a number of administrative barriers to investment, officials and business people believed that progress was too slow. Each step in the list of barriers to investment had its own history and its own constituency. Some steps in the red tape resulted from what the report called "over-legislation." Some problems were also attributed to decision-making rules that reflected political connections, personal loyalties, family affiliations, and simply job security. Many of the problems that investors faced were the results of deeply ingrained attitudes in the ministries and agencies involved. Moreover, "invisible social and political cues," as the report said, can be more important than visible written rules, and these can be special barriers to foreigners, who do not understand them quickly. Action required modification of legislation and regulations, but also more difficult changes in how bureaucrats thought about foreign investment. Solutions had to be tailored to the history, bureaucratic interests, and institutional context of each step in the process and they had to tackle basic attitudes. There would have to be some kind of constant pressure within government for reform if changes were to be effected. The three steps against red tape had helped, but more was needed.

The opportunity for adding another step was to come from a "mega-project." The idea was to use a "live case" as a way to generate workable solutions on the spot, when problems were actually being encountered by an investor. The officials involved in solving problems for this case would, it was hoped, also continue to press for change, even after the particular project was in operation. Two conditions for success were clear at the outset: first, the project chosen for the case approach had to be one that was very important to top government officials, because their constant backing would be required, and second, the company sponsoring the project would have to be willing to commit a significant amount of management time and resources to making the approach succeed.

A Mega-Opportunity

As the Mozambican government generated a vision of how the country might develop, one of the goals that had emerged was the attraction of a small number of "mega-projects." These would be very large projects that would demonstrate to other investors that Mozambique was a good place to do business. Further, mega-projects would support medium- and small-scale local firms as suppliers, which in turn would encourage expansion of the informal sector. But the administrative barriers for a mega-project appeared overwhelming. Establishing such a project would require the approval and cooperation of a number of ministries and state-owned enterprises. Since the decisions would be important, they could not easily be delegated to low-level officials. Moreover, negotiating an arrangement that would benefit the country would require coordination on the part of all these institutions. In some of these, suspicions of foreign investors were particularly deeply entrenched. Even if the basic approvals and terms could be agreed, implementing the project would require still further cooperation by many ministries, agencies, state-owned enterprises, and local government units.

One potential mega-project had already become mired in the process of obtaining approvals. At least since the mid-1950s, the north of the country had been known to contain significant gas fields. Developing them would require a pipeline and a market. The

South African oil company Sasol obtained a claim on the fields from the Ministry of Mineral Resources and Energy and proposed piping gas to South Africa, where the gas could substitute for coal to produce gasoline in Sasol's South African plants. But discussion of the project dragged on, with no resolution. In 1995, the ministry concluded a Heads of Agreement that gave the rights that had been held by Sasol to Enron, a U.S. company. Enron proposed building a pipeline from the fields to Maputo and putting together a group of investors to build an export-oriented iron and steel facility there. Although the ministry claimed that Sasol's rights had expired, Sasol disagreed and protested the assignment. With the new dispute, it appeared unlikely that this project would get off the ground quickly.[13] The need for a better mechanism for negotiating and implementing large projects was becoming apparent.

Another potential mega-project appeared in 1995, when Gencor, a South African minerals company, contacted the government about the possibility of building an aluminum smelter in Mozambique. Since the government wanted to avoid the problems that other investors had experienced, it was ready for a new approach. The approach that eventually emerged comprised a two-tier structure for negotiation and a three-tier structure to solve problems in implementation.

This approach became the *fourth step* in what turned out to be a program of complementary steps to attack red tape in Mozambique. This step was to solve problems for the investor by speeding the negotiations and the implementation of the resulting agreement, and it ended up institutionalizing a model for future negotiations of large projects. And by focusing on the problems faced in an actual case of investment, it accomplished the goal of establishing practical solutions for some red-tape problems and empowering a number of officials who could assist future investors and continue to dismantle unnecessary red-tape in the system.

The detailed lessons for other countries are presented at the end of this study. They are easier to understand with a grasp of how the case-based approached worked in practice.

2

The Proposed Aluminum Smelter

The Project

Gencor, the company that proposed the aluminum smelter, already smelted aluminum at Richards Bay in South Africa.[14] The company was optimistic about the world market for aluminum and wanted to become a "major player" in the industry.[15] According to its projections, Western demand for aluminum would grow by around 2.4% per year until the year 2005. This would amount to an annual increase in demand of around 420,000 tons. Growth could be even greater, if one counted on the emerging economies of Asia, such as India and China. The company predicted that the average London Metal Exchange price for aluminum ingot for the next ten years would be about US$1,750 per ton (in December 1996 dollars).[16] Although the market appeared to offer profitable growth opportunities for Gencor, the company could not expand capacity at Richards Bay beyond the new Hillside smelter that was close to completion. As a result, the company began to look for another site to add more capacity.

The company's goal was to build a new smelter that could produce 245,000 tons of aluminum annually by 2001; further, it wanted to be able to double the capacity of the new smelter in the future, should market conditions remain favorable. This would mean that the company would eventually hold about 5% of world smelting capacity.

At the outset, the proposed plant would be a half-sized clone[17] of Gencor's Hillside aluminum smelter in Richards Bay. It would use know-how from the French company Aluminium Pechiney, similar to that used at Hillside.[18] The smelter would import 480,000 tons of alumina per year from Australia (where an affiliate mined and refined bauxite) convert the alumina to aluminum, and export aluminum ingot.[19] The project would cost around US$1.3 billion.

Several reasons led company managers to consider Mozambique as a possible site for expansion. First, Maputo, Mozambique's capital, offered a good harbor, critical for the volumes of alumina to be imported and aluminum to be exported.[20] Second, in October 1995 Eskom, the South African utility company supplying Richards Bay, had stated its willingness to provide electricity at a competitive price if Gencor built a smelter in Mozambique.[21] The cost of electricity, which typically accounted for about 20–25% of the operating costs of an aluminum smelter, was the principal factor that differentiated a low-cost aluminum smelter from a high-cost one.[22] Location near Maputo would allow the necessary 435 MW of electricity to be transmitted from the existing Eskom grid through two new lines from South Africa.[23] Eskom projected 5,000 MW of excess capacity when the project might go on-stream; it also had mothballed plants with an additional 3,600 MW of capacity. Negotiations between Eskom and the Mozambicans could, however, lead to the eventual purchase by Eskom of electricity from the Mozambican Cahora Bassa dam and the possibility of expansion by building another dam downstream on the Zambesi River at Mepanda Uncua. This potential would be especially appealing to the Mozambican government. Third, tariff preferences favored location in Mozambique. Since Mozambique was an "Asia-Pacific-Caribbean (APC) country" under the Lomé Agreement, primary aluminum produced there could enter the European Union duty free, while the Union's common external tariff imposed a 6% charge on aluminum from elsewhere. Finally, Gencor believed that the South African Industrial Development Corporation (IDC), a corporation owned by the South African government, would offer low-cost finance and guarantees for South African investors in Mozambique.[24]

With these advantages of Mozambique in mind, in December 1995 I. Reid and M. Oberholzer[25] of Gencor visited Deputy Minister R. Jusob in the Ministry of Industry, Commerce, and Tourism (MICTUR) in Maputo to discuss locating a smelter in Mozambique. The company managers proposed an agreement to cover tax, land tenure, import and export duties, and infrastructure, to be concluded by November 1996. With an agreement, the company could seek funding, and construction would start in 1997. In the meeting, the managers provided estimates of needs for water, waste disposal, road and rail links, telecommunications, and electricity for the construction phase.

Enthusiasm on the part of Mozambicans was immediate. By any standards, the project was a large one, but it was especially large in comparison to the size of the Mozambican economy.[26] The investment fit into the national goal of attracting a mega-project and promised opportunities for local suppliers. The sponsoring company's experience in developing local suppliers in South Africa could help it in providing similar assistance to small businesses in Mozambique. Although the aluminum would be exported largely as ingot, plans could include an industrial park to encourage the manufacture of aluminum products near the smelter, as well as to house support industries. Subsequent projections by the International Finance Corporation (IFC) indicated that the project would add more than 7% per year to Mozambique's GDP in its early years, contribute about US$61 million per year to net foreign exchange earnings, and directly increase tax receipts by about 2% of revenues. The smelter might employ about 5,000 people during the construction stage. Perhaps half of the workers could be Mozambicans. The company predicted 873 permanent jobs in the operating plant, of which 793 could be held by Mozambicans. The IFC estimated that local procurement would possibly create an additional 2,600 jobs.[27]

Although Mozambican officials wanted the investment, never before had the government succeeded in negotiating a project of anything like this scale.[28]

Stumbling Blocks

The aluminum smelter project, or Mozal,[29] as both the project and the subsidiary company came to be known, faced hurdles from the outset. A foreign investment of more than $100 million required an Investment Project Authorization (Autorização de Projecto de Investimento, or IPA) from the Council of Ministers before it could proceed. But ministers were too busy to negotiate such an agreement, and on some issues their ministries held conflicting views that would have to be resolved.

Issues would have to be settled with all the ministries and agencies affected before any document could be submitted to the Council of Ministers. The Mozal project would, for example, require an agreement on tax status and customs status; eventually a number of permits would be needed for construction of plant and housing; moreover, since government-owned enterprises were involved, separate agreements would have to cover access to port facilities, possible rail transportation, road construction, water, sewers, and electric power. Land tenure was complicated in Mozambique; since the project would require access to large tracts of land, government involvement was essential. Moreover, complicated arrangements with the government would have to be devised for the resettlement of people on land to be used for the project. In fact, the land issue was so important that the company asked in its first meetings with government that potential sites be reserved immediately and held for the company until March 1997, when it proposed making a "go or no-go" decision. Since the project could have a significant impact on the environment, approval from the ministry concerned with the environment would be necessary. Similarly, an agreement on labor would have to be concluded with the relevant ministry. And on and on. The company knew that investors and lenders for the project would not make firm commitments until the basic agreement and the important subsidiary agreements and various permits and approvals were in place.

The issues for a huge smelter were sufficiently complex and important that negotiation would inevitably involve high-level people from each of the many affected ministries and agencies. Yet, if Mozal negotiated directly with each of the relevant government units, the process promised to be extremely drawn out. And one ministry or agency might be able to block the whole project, as appeared to have happened at least temporarily with the gas pipeline and steel plant.

Uncoordinated negotiations raised problems for the government, as well. It was unlikely that ministry-by-ministry negotiations would lead to an optimum agreement for Mozambique. Individual ministries would give too much or too little, depending on their own views of the project. There would be no clear mechanism, while negotiations were proceeding, for the government to weigh the total package of terms being offered by individual ministries and agencies. Presumably, some kind of judgment on the entire proposed agreement would be made at the Council of Ministers level, where the final decision would be issued. But, if the individually negotiated terms seemed to add up to an inappropriate agreement, the draft might be rejected at that level and negotiations would be extended for still longer.[30] Neither party wanted this kind of protracted discussion.

The next two and a half months were frustrating for company managers. They encountered problems arranging and holding appointments with the many agencies that had to approve parts of the project and they received no commitments at all from officials. Some light appeared in early March 1996. The company chairman, R. Barbour, invited O. Baloi, Minister of Industry, Commerce, and Tourism, to visit the opening ceremony in April for the company's second smelter, Hillside, at Richards Bay. Also in early March, Barbour traveled to Maputo and met with a number of ministers[31] and the chairman of the state-owned enterprise that ran the railroads and ports. In each case, he described the proposed project and presented the needs of the company that were relevant to the minister: reservation of sites, infrastructure, tax incentives, exemptions from duties, and freedom for foreign exchange transactions. While he was in Maputo, Barbour also met with officials from the U.S. Embassy and the World Bank. A World Bank official suggested contact with its private financing arm, the International Finance Corporation.

Barbour attempted to reduce the problem of arranging meetings in the future by asking each minister to name a contact person for the company for its dealings with his ministry. Minister Baloi named M. Mbeve, a National Director in the ministry.[32] At the same time, the Investment Promotion Center (CPI) became involved. This organization was charged with assisting potential investors in the country. Mbeve (named by the minister) and F. Sumbana and, eventually, H. Dombo (both of the CPI) were to play major roles in this project and in paving the way for subsequent investment.

In fact, Mozambique had in place a structure that was supposed to overcome exactly the kinds of problems posed by this kind of negotiation with foreign investors. The Investment Promotion Center (CPI) saw its major role as providing service to prospective investors by assisting them through the process. It had created an Evaluation Commission, which met at the CPI monthly to look at projects where special issues arose. This Commission was made up of representatives of the tutelary ministry for the project under discussion (in the case of Mozal, this would be the Ministry of Industry, Commerce, and Tourism), the central bank, the Customs and the Tax Departments of the Ministry of Planning and Finance, the Ministry for the Environment, the Ministry of Transportation and Communications, and the Ministry of Labor.

The Commission had worked satisfactorily for some fairly large projects in the past. Coca-Cola's project (some $20 million of investment) had been handled by the Commission, for example. On the other hand, what had earlier seemed large now looked small, in comparison to the smelter. Moreover, Coca-Cola's project had not required that the Commission consider anything that departed from or lay outside the normal rules. No really difficult decisions had been involved.

As interest in the smelter grew, the proposal was indeed discussed at the CPI's Evaluation Commission, but problems arose almost immediately. The idea of declaring the smelter area to be a free-trade zone was challenged by the representatives of Customs and the Ministry of Labor, for example. Although, the law allowed the negotiation of special incentives for a project of more than $500 million, the officials normally attending the meetings of the Evaluation Commission were not sufficiently senior that they could make decisions with such major implications. The Investment Promotion Center quickly realized that the issues in this case were too difficult and important to be decided by the government representatives on the Commission. Moreover, the Evaluation Commission had other projects to deal with; if it were to tackle something as difficult and complicated as Mozal, progress was bound to be slow and would affect other investments. The company wanted to move fast; and the government did not want to delay this or other investors and thus confirm its reputation for red tape.

By early April, company managers were again becoming frustrated. Evidence was accumulating that their November target date for an agreement had been overly optimistic. They had not even received permission to carry out tests at potential sites. Difficult issues had not been faced at all. Oberholzer complained to Mbeve: "Without a turnaround in performance, it will be difficult for our feasibility study team to make a confident recommendation to the Board of Directors."

All parties were recognizing that the existing way of negotiating the Investment Project Authorization and the many necessary associated agreements was likely to mean no agreement for this kind of large and complicated project for a very long time, if ever.

Both company managers and government officials believed that something new was required. Despite this consensus, more ups and downs were to come; even reaching the basic agreement was not to be easy.

3

Moving toward Agreement

Creating a Structure

The new structure that the parties assembled for negotiating the basic agreements for the Mozal project was relatively simple.[33] (See Figure 3 on page 116.)

Minister Baloi had proposed the creation of an Inter-ministerial Task Force to oversee the Mozal negotiations. This Task Force comprised the ministers whose interests were most affected by the project and whose cooperation was essential for the smelter to be constructed and operated: Baloi himself and the ministers from Planning and Finance, Public Works and Housing, and Mineral Resources and Energy. Membership was flexible, however, and the Task Force could invite other ministers when issues affecting their interests were to be discussed. The Task Force was to be chaired by Minister Baloi, since the smelter was an industrial project and thus fell under the tutelary function of the Ministry of Industry, Commerce, and Tourism.

Since ministers did not have the time to work out all the details that were involved in solving problems facing a potential investor—even in the negotiation stage—a decision was made that later proved very important: a formal second-tier structure was created. Following the model just established, ministers named high-level repre-

FIGURE 1
Coordinating Structure for Negotiations

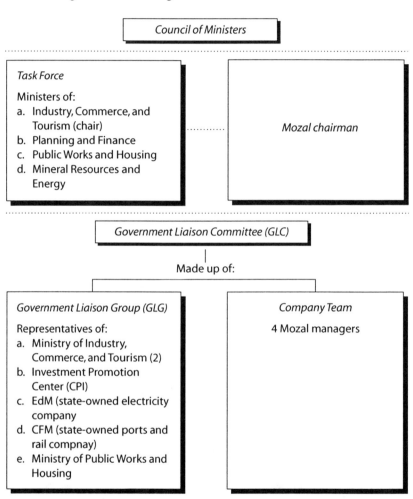

Council of Ministers

Task Force

Ministers of:
a. Industry, Commerce, and
   Tourism (chair)
b. Planning and Finance
c. Public Works and Housing
d. Mineral Resources and
   Energy

Mozal chairman

Government Liaison Committee (GLC)

Made up of:

Government Liaison Group (GLG)

Representatives of:
a. Ministry of Industry,
   Commerce, and Tourism (2)
b. Investment Promotion
   Center (CPI)
c. EdM (state-owned electricity
   company
d. CFM (state-owned ports and
   rail compnay)
e. Ministry of Public Works and
   Housing

Company Team

4 Mozal managers

sentatives from their ministries to represent them in the Government Liaison Group, which was to be dedicated solely to the Mozal negotiations and headed by Mbeve, from the Ministry of Industry, Commerce, and Tourism (MICTUR). The early group comprised Mbeve and J. Moyane, from MICTUR; F. Sumbana, from the Investment Promotion Center,[34] and C. Veloso, from the state-owned electricity company (EdM).[35] Alternates would be named to attend when the principal member had to be absent. Soon representatives of a few other organizations became regular attendees. These included the state-owned ports and railroad company (CFM) and the Ministry for Public Works and Housing.

The company formed counterpart structures. The chairman of Mozal, R. Barbour, would deal directly with the chairman of the Task Force. They would meet on an "as needed" basis to discuss broad policy issues, not the more tedious details that would be handled at the second tier. A company team was named to meet with the Government Liaison Group. This team consisted of four managers, headed initially by Oberholzer (later by P. Cowie, when he took up residence in Mozambique and became responsible for government affairs). The Government Liaison Group and the company team together would form the Government Liaison Committee (GLC).

Officially, this Committee was to:

a. Expedite official procedures, decision-making, permits, and approvals.

b. Coordinate between all government and local departments and authorities.

c. Evaluate and discuss progress to sensitize all attendees to the important issues.

d. Assist in whatever way is possible.

e. Report to the Council of Ministers as and when deemed necessary.[36]

In fact, the Government Liaison Committee was to become the principal negotiating body. Its members would report to their superiors and receive instructions from them with respect to major issues that had to be decided. The draft Investment Project Authorization would have to emerge out of this key Committee, for approval by the company's board, the Task Force, and eventually the Council of Ministers. And the Committee would exercise influence over the negotiation of the individual infrastructure and other agreements that would together make up the basic agreements required for the project to proceed.

Concluding the Heads of Agreement

The Government Liaison Committee met for the first time on May 29, 1996, but it was not quite clear how the Committee should proceed. It had no precedents to which it could turn. The eventual goal was an Investment Project Authorization (IPA), but rather than trying to conclude a complicated IPA immediately, the Committee accepted the idea of trying first to negotiate a "Heads of Agreement." This document would set out in brief, non-technical language the resolution of the major issues involved in the project. Once the principles had been agreed, the group could move on to work out all the details for the IPA.

With no previous agreement as a model, the Committee decided that the Heads of Agreement would cover the tax and duty regime, the land concession, exchange control and repatriation of profits, infrastructure (including harbor, right of way for power lines and roads, water supply, storm water and sewerage), and any other issues desired by either side. In the case of infrastructure, there would eventually have to be separate agreements with the state-owned companies, but the Heads of Agreement would set out some principles and government commitments.

In late July 1996, the company submitted to the Committee its first draft of the Heads of Agreement. With a document on the table, optimism on both sides increased, and the Minister of Mineral Resources and Energy told a Mozambican news agency in early August that the company would start building the smelter during the next year, and that a second dam would be built on the Zambezi River to support the power from Cahora Bassa.

But serious problems remained for the negotiators. One critical problem was agreeing on the basic status of the project. The draft Heads of Agreement proposed that the project be designated as an Industrial Free Zone (IFZ). The recently passed free-trade zone legislation would give the company important tax and duty exemptions. It appeared, however, that the Customs and Tax Departments might challenge any such exemptions.

Since the smelter would import most of its needs and export its product, some way of avoiding duties was essential. The legislation for free-trade zones allowed duty-free import of construction materials, equipment, and materials.[37] To be eligible for zone status under the legislation, a company had to export at least 80% of its output; this was not a problem. There were, however, other ways of handling the duties. In theory, an exporting firm could pay duties on its imports and then apply for a rebate upon export of the finished product. To the company, however, this was not an attractive option. First, it would have to tie up working capital in duties. Second, procedures for obtaining duty refunds were notoriously slow and bureaucratic—in Mozambique, as in many other countries. Since the value of imported raw materials loomed large in this project, managers considered the ability to import free of duty as extremely important.

In addition, Mozambique's legislation for Industrial Free Zones offered tax provisions that were attractive to the company. One option under the law was that a company declared as a free-zone enterprise would pay a one percent tax on its sales, in lieu of taxes on income and dividends.[38] Moreover, the free-zone regulations provided for as much as a five-year holiday from this tax and granted an IFZ company exemption from exchange controls.[39]

Although the legislation for IFZs was in place, the government had yet to issue an IFZ certificate to any firm; moreover, the new law left many details uncovered. Customs officials were doubtful, and the tax office was reluctant to see such a potentially large source of tax revenue receive this kind of incentive. Even the central bank began to express concerns, as well.

The Investment Promotion Center's facilitating role became especially important in the resulting discussions. With customs and tax departments and the central bank still questioning the arrangement, the Investment Promotion Center arranged a special meeting in late August with representatives of the National Directorate of Taxation and Auditing and the central bank. The meeting resulted in acceptance of the principle of free-zone status.[40] The company agreed to the tax of one percent on its sales and to a limit on any tax holiday to one year after the start of commercial production began.

Other paragraphs of the draft Heads of Agreement committed the government to facilitate cooperation between the Mozambican electricity company (EdM) and the South African power company (Eskom) for a power agreement and to help with necessary permits. The company would be exempt from other taxes, and special tax incentives would be offered for expatriate staff. The government would assure a certain channel depth in the harbor and priority for Mozal ships in obtaining berths. Since the exact site for the smelter remained uncertain, the Heads of Agreement mentioned two possible sites at or very near the port, but left the issue open.

By late August, major substantive issues seemed to have been resolved and a new draft of the Heads of Agreement was prepared and submitted to the Council of Ministers for approval. After 90 minutes of debate, the Council sent the draft back for more negotiations. As if that weren't enough bad news for the company, the Council also granted permission for a study of another potential smelter project, by Reynolds. The study would be financed by the U.S. government and the promoters had hired as consultants a group from within the state-owned electricity company. Mozal received one piece of good news, however: the Council gave explicit authorization to the state-owned electricity company in Mozambique to negotiate an agreement with the South African company, something Mozal had sought for months.

It turned out that the choice of site had been a major issue in the discussions by the Council. The company strongly preferred locating very near the port, in one of the two sites mentioned in the draft Heads of Agreement, to minimize transport costs. Officials from the Office of Physical Planning within the Ministry of Planning and Finance and the state-owned port and rail company (CFM), however, argued that the Maputo port area was already congested; the large area required for a smelter was simply not available. As a backup, the company had proposed the second site, only a few kilometers away. The government objected to this alternative, as well. Since the area was rather densely settled, taking land for the smelter there would require expensive and politically unpopular relocation of a large number of people.

In response to the objections, the company investigated eight additional possible sites. In November, the company agreed to give up the proposed sites near the harbor and focused its attention on "Site K," some 17 kilometers away, near the toll road being constructed to run from Johannesburg, South Africa, to Maputo.[41] Site K was agreeable to both the government and the company.

Still other issues were emerging. The new choice of site meant that more infrastructure would be required, but the government lacked the funds. The company was going to have to finance the increased costs. As a result, company managers proposed that Mozal be allowed to subtract from the taxes it would pay over the first eight years an amount up to $15 million for expenditures on infrastructure that would be open to the public.[42] This proposal went into the draft Heads of Agreement. The company also asked for assurances from the government on security issues, but government representatives found the proposals unacceptable. The price of land became an issue in the on-going discussions. As the number of issues multiplied, the company suggested that additional representatives be invited to the discussions, to deal with matters concerning environment, physical planning, and roads.

Another very serious problem appeared, one of a quite different kind. Oberholzer began to worry that the company board and legal staff might, in the end, reject what the Council would approve. From company headquarters, managers and lawyers were insisting on more detail to cover issues left open in the draft, and they wanted tighter legal language. Further, other potential investors in the project had their own ideas of what kinds of assurances should be in the Heads of Agreement. In contrast to the home office, company managers located in Mozambique tended to see the issues as adequately covered or not worth the long discussions that would be generated if issues were re-opened. As a result, a new set of negotiations began, this time inside the company and between the company and other investors. Managers spent much of September trying to settle issues within the corporate structure.

Meanwhile, still another problem threatened: the price of aluminum had fallen from around $1,750 to $1,200, as Eastern European aluminum was sold on the Western market. If lower prices were to persist, the whole economics of the project might have to be revisited. The mood was not good.

Nevertheless, some things began to look up. Progress had been made in the Committee to resolve issues that had bothered the Council of Ministers when it had considered the earlier version of the Heads of Agreement. The more positive atmosphere was reflected in a successful cocktail party held at a local hotel. The event was attended by government officials involved in the negotiations, local mayors, and representatives from the state-owned telephone, telecommunications, and ports companies, from the World Bank, the South African embassy, a construction company, and local companies, as well as from KPMG, which provided advisory services to the company. Further, at the end of November, the Mozambican prime minister and a number of other government officials visited Richards Bay, at the invitation of the company. For a brief period, managers even feared that the negotiations with the government were going too fast; they seemed to be running ahead of the discussions inside the company and with potential investors.

In early December 1966, there was enough consensus that the Government Liaison Committee sent another version of the Heads of Agreement to the Inter-ministerial Task Force. The new draft proposed site-K and it included the modified tax provisions. It altered somewhat the government commitments on power, harbor access, and the harbor channel, and road and rail links, and dropped the insistence on absolute priority on berths for ships. Other technical concerns, such as which language version ruled, were dealt with more precisely.

The Task Force, whose members had been kept informed of changes by the Government Liaison Group, approved the draft and sent the document on to the Council of Ministers. This time the Council of Ministers gave its okay. Company headquarters accepted it as well, and the Heads of Agreement was signed on March 20, 1997, after some delays in finding a signing date suitable for all parties.[43] A major milestone had been reached.

Although the original schedule had proved optimistic, the negotiations had nevertheless proceeded quickly. Less than six months had elapsed between completion of the first draft and the submission of the final version to the Task Force.

Negotiating the Subsidiary Agreements

While the Government Liaison Committee was negotiating the Heads of Agreement, it was also working on other issues. These ran from solving low-level bureaucratic problems—such as difficulties managers faced in getting multiple entry visas for which they had paid, unofficial charges imposed on managers when they left the country, and problems in getting telephone service to the company office—to discussions of the subsidiary agreements that would have to be in place for the project to proceed.

The power agreements were especially complicated. The arrangement would have to include the South African state-owned power company (Eskom), the Mozambican state-owned power company (EdM), which held a monopoly on electricity distribution within the country, and the Swazi power company (SEB), since one of the two power lines would pass through Swaziland. It was eventually decided that a new consortium company would have to be formed to handle the transmission of power, the Mozambican Transmission Company (Motraco). Any such arrangement raised foreign policy issues that seemed to go beyond the authority of EdM to decide. Even after the Council had in August given authority to EdM to negotiate an agreement for transmitting power from the South African grid and to provide power for the construction stage, those discussions dragged on. The complexity was increased by the hope on the part of Mozambicans that some of the power would come from an increase in sales from Cahora Bassa and the potential new dam downstream on the Zambesi River.

In spite of the discussions, by the time the Heads of Agreement was signed, none of the subsidiary agreements had been completed. Agreements still had to be reached on power during construction, power during operation, labor, potable water, raw water, sewerage, the harbor and port, and the critical Land Use Plan and Relocation Plan. But meetings with the relevant parties had begun. The Government Liaison Committee had established a positive, problem-solving attitude that would spill over into most of the discussions of subsidiary agreements; and the Committee was ready to intervene if necessary to accelerate progress.

Conduct of Meetings

The speed with which the Heads of Agreement was concluded was due at least partly to the way meetings had been conducted. Initially, meetings of the Government Liaison Committee were to be convened at least every second week. Further, working sessions could be held outside the regular meeting schedule. In fact, the Committee had met ten times during the negotiations for the Heads of Agreement. Some of the meetings were held in Maputo; others, in Richards Bay.[44] Officials who were not members of the Committee were invited to specific meetings, as the agenda required. The meetings were conducted in English, but a translator was always present to help with language problems.

With experience, the members of the Government Liaison Committee developed a pattern. To encourage thought and preparation, an agenda was circulated to all invitees before each meeting. The agenda was built by having the company and the government each list five issues that they thought were particularly important for the meeting. After the meeting, KPMG, advisors to Mozal, prepared detailed minutes, which reported who attended, who was invited but absent, the issues discussed, and the understandings reached. And, each government member reported—some in writing—the results of the meeting to his minister or equivalent. On occasion, these reports included issues that the minister had to decide, or which had to be dealt with by the Task Force, since agreement required resolving different positions held by different ministries or agencies. The reactions of the ministers or the Task Force provided inputs for the next meeting of the Liaison Group.

With only minor changes, the structure and procedures were to remain intact for the next stage, the completion of the basic Investment Project Authorization.

4

Completing the Negotiations

Concluding the Investment Project Authorization (IPA)

Since the approved Heads of Agreement covered the important terms governing the smelter project, everyone believed that it would be easy to move to the Investment Project Authorization, which would spell out in detail what had been accepted in principle. Negotiations began again in earnest in June 1997, but progress was much slower than anticipated.

By November, two issues remained as visible blocks to progress; they involved foreign exchange and the employment of expatriates. Dombo (of the Investment Promotion Center), who had joined the Government Liaison Group and was playing an increasingly important role in solving problems, asked Mbeve for help in organising another meeting with officials from the central bank. A meeting was similarly arranged with the Minister of Labor. Both of these issues were resolved in these special meetings of company managers, the technical people, and members of the Government Liaison Group.

A draft Investment Project Authorization was submitted to the company's board in early December. Again, as with the Heads of Agreement, problems appeared at company headquarters. The company board considered the draft a "major disappointment to us after six months of negotiations." Headquarters provided counter-proposals that would re-open discussions of issues that seemed to have been settled. As a result, Dombo and company managers held numerous meetings to resolve differences and to try to satisfy the corporate head office. Discussions dealt with issues such as the lease period on Maputo harbor. Mozal headquarters had also reopened the issue of granting priority for berthing of vessels bringing supplies to Mozal, a preference that the state-owned harbor and railroad company had refused to accept. On this issue, a meeting of the minds was reached when the parties agreed to a "first planned, first berthed" principle, which was incorporated into the Investment Project Authorization.

The revised Investment Project Authorization, containing compromises on a number of such issues, was submitted to the Council of Ministers, which approved it on December 23, 1997, two years after the company's managers first visited the Ministry of Industry, Commerce, and Tourism. The prime minister signed the document in January 1998.

Completing the Subsidiary Agreements

By January 1998, with one exception—the first stage of the power agreement, completed in March 1997—none of the subsidiary agreements had been completed; arrangements for harbor, telecommunications, labor, water, sewerage all remained to be concluded. And the Land Use Plan, the Relocation Plan, and road layouts had not been approved. The board of Billiton, by now the name of the principal investor and sponsor,[45] met on January 21 and decided that it would not authorize going ahead with the project at that time, and would postpone any final decision at least until the harbor and electricity supply agreements were in place. Managers from a potential Japanese investor refused to carry the decision to the company board at all until these agreements were complete.

In February, a Labor Agreement was signed with the Ministry of Labor. It turned out that this had not presented major difficulties. With a completed Investment Project Authorization and one more important agreement in place, everyone was encouraged.

Given the importance of electricity, the company focused its attention on completing this agreement. Management asked the Government Liaison Committee to help expedite the process.

In February, the Mozambican power company signed an agreement for power during the construction stage. Although progress on the basic agreements had been encouraging, detailed agreements for power supply remained elusive. The new company (Montraco) was still to be formed and its partners wanted the entity to be granted Industrial Free Zone status. Any arrangement with Motraco remained contingent on new approval by the Council. Eventually, Mbeve was asked to try to intervene to seek a resolution from the Council of Ministers. In April 1998, the Council approved the critical Investment Project Authorization for Motraco, granting it Industrial Free Zone status. This broke a barrier and the all-important electricity agreements could be concluded.

In spite of the fact that not every subsidiary agreement was in place, the breakthrough on the power arrangements led Billiton to decide that it could seek commitments from other investors and it announced its own "go-ahead" decision in May 1998. On October 30, the company reported that the financing had been assembled. Billiton would provide 47% of the equity, another 24% would come from the Industrial Development Corporation of South Africa, and 25% would be provided by Mitsubishi of Japan. The Mozambique Government would own 4%, with its contribution financed by a loan from the European Investment Bank. Debt would include both senior and subordinated debt, which would carry fixed minimum and variable incremental interest payments.[46] The project finances were contributed as shown in Table 1.

Discussions of the other agreements, however, dragged on. Finishing the final harbor agreement was to prove especially difficult. In January, it had looked as if most of the terms had been agreed;

Table 1. Financing of Mozal

Investor/lender	Country	Amount (million USD)
Equity		
Industrial Development Corporation of South Africa (IDC)	South Africa	125
Billiton	United Kingdom	245
Mitsubishi	Japan	130
Government of Mozambique	Mozambique	20
Debt		
IDC	South Africa	380
Coface	France	110
IFC[a]	Multilateral	120
Development Bank of South Africa (DBSA)	South Africa	70
Commonwealth Development Corporation (CDC)	United Kingdom	55
European Investment Bank	Europe	40
PROPARCO	France	25
Deutsche Investitions-und Entwicklungs- Gesellschaft mbH	Germany	20
Total		1,340

Source: Data provided by Mozal.

a. This was the largest commitment to a single project ever made by the International Finance Corporation. The private investors viewed participation by the World Bank Group as increasing the protection of the project from arbitrary government action. The IFC's analysis indicated break-even at a price of US$1,493 per ton for full costs (with depreciation and finance charges including base interest on subordinated debt) in the third year, declining to $1,070 in the eleventh year. It estimated a financial return of 13.7% for the project at its base price forecast of $1,750 per ton.

the cost of onboard stevedoring seemed to be the only significant source of continuing disagreement. Consequently, an agreement was announced in April 1998 to cover Maputo harbor. The company, however, then decided that it would be better to operate out of new facilities in Matola, which was less crowded and more easily accessible from the new smelter site. Thus, Mozal wanted to construct port facilities at this alternative site, near Maputo. It did not object to ownership of the facilities by the port and railroad company. An addendum to the earlier contract was agreed in August 1998 to shift from Maputo's harbor to nearby Matola. The expectation at the time was that the state company, CFM, would operate the facilities and be paid a reduced fee for its services (lower than its published tariffs, to compensate for the fact that the company was paying the cost of the new facilities), but eventually Mozal proposed that the port be operated by a private party. CFM was agreeable, but still wanted at least part of the fee that it was to be paid under the original arrangements.[47] The final agreement was completed in August 1998 by an addendum to the earlier document.

Mozal had negotiated directly with CFM, as an independent state-owned enterprise.[48] CFM even had its own legal department. Although the negotiations were direct, the Government Liaison Committee was kept informed of the discussions and apparently had an influence on attitudes, because of its strong support of the project.

While the port issue was clearly very complicated, seemingly simple matters had also turned out to be extremely difficult. One of the most bothersome subsidiary contracts was the one for water supply, even though the amount of water required for the project was not considered large.[49] In fact, this was one of the first agreements to be discussed; discussions were already underway in December 1996. But, the agreement turned out to be the last to be concluded. Part of the difficulty was that the water company had major problems elsewhere, with broken pipes, periodic cholera outbreaks, and so on. As a result, it was hard to get management attention to the contract. And, once one version was signed, the company had to go back for modifications, as Mozal's lenders abroad demanded specific provisions on assignment of the contract, should lenders have to foreclose on the company. Again, it proved difficult to get management attention to what seemed to be a small matter. Mozal managers had to depend on help from members of the Government Liaison Group to push for attention. Final agreement remained outstanding until early 1999.

Deciding on the basic Relocation Plan for people living in the area where the smelter was to be built had not raised difficult issues. But implementing it had, as funds seemed to go unaccounted for, some displaced families viewed their replacement housing as inappropriate, and new claims on land regularly appeared. Issues concerning relocation were repeatedly dealt with by the Committee, which kept the process moving.

The project had to receive approval for a Land Use Plan, as well, which would re-zone agricultural land to industrial and residential use. The approval was, it was believed, to come from the Council of Ministers. But the role of the local governor and of the Ministry of Internal Affairs in approving the Plan was not clear. Discussions seemed to go in a circle about who had to approve this document first. As a result, approval was to be postponed regularly; it was not received until early 1999. Similarly, approval for access roads had to await final decisions on the exact location of sections of the toll road being constructed from South Africa to Maputo. This involved co-ordination with several ministries and agencies as well as with the foreign company that was building the road, and discussions dragged on and on.

Another time-consuming problem was finding appropriate sites for expatriate housing. Several locations had come to the attention of company management. But as government permits were sought for the sites the company was willing to consider, some barrier always appeared. The government suggested alternatives, but these were not appropriate in the company's view. The issue was also to run on into the implementation stage before it was finally resolved.

Preparing for Implementation

When it appeared that the major agreements would indeed fall in place, the Government Liaison Committee began steps that would help in actually implementing the project. For example, meetings were held with the Investment Promotion Center to generate proposals for the tax authorities on how to handle suppliers to the project. These led to discussions about procedures for registering contractors.

As the many upcoming problems of implementation became clearer, a system of Task Groups began to grow, first informally and then more formally. These groups met to facilitate the resolution of issues concerning customs, land use, and harbor, for example. Task Groups dealt with immigration, customs, ticket processing, and even access to lounges at the airport. As their roles grew, the Task Groups began to give regular reports to the monthly Government Liaison Committee meetings. The result was the involvement of many more people, from both the government and the company, in moving the project along.

Lessons Learned

Negotiating the basic agreements had been difficult, but the joint committee approach had worked. The company had received the first Industrial Free Zone certificate to be handed out by Mozambique. The Investment Project Authorization was certainly the most complicated to have been negotiated in the country. And almost all the troublesome subsidiary agreements had been concluded.

The negotiations for the basic agreements generated a great deal of experience that was to affect the next stage. At this point at least four factors seemed important in explaining the success and would be carried over to the next stage:

First, the formal structure was built around a core of high-level government officials who had become deeply committed to solving problems. Mbeve, chairman of the Committee, was described by J. Ceron,[50] an advisor to the Investment Promotion Center, as someone with the background of an "apparatchik," but with none of the attributes in practice that one associates with the term. He chaired the Committee "with a prudent hand, always looking to broker solutions for the government and Mozal, when troubles were on the horizon." The description went on: "Although he could be considered a member of the 'old guard,' certainly his attitude represented the 'new Mozambique.'" He was described as "the architect of the consensus process." Sumbana, the director of the Investment Promotion Center (CPI) held an American MBA and had come to the CPI from the private sector in Mozambique. This gave him a special ability to bridge the government and business interface. Moreover, he was committed to converting the CPI from a screening agency and barrier to investment into an effective promotion agency, a task in which he was succeeding, although few directors elsewhere had been able to do so. Dombo had come to the Investment Promotion Center from another government agency where he had been involved largely with agriculture. Ceron described him as having "a keen sense of humor, many times utilizing this personality trait to appease and smooth conflict situations," and as having "a steel-like resolve to move things forward." The same commentator said: "in retrospect, it is difficult to imagine the Mozal process moving forward as it did without these two characteristics he brought to the table." Other members of the Task Force showed similar dedication. In short the process involved a rather exceptional group of committed government officials with the determination to succeed.

Second, the company had provided a well-liked and respected resident manager for the Mozambique Affairs team. Cowie was a South African who had gained confidence with headquarters management by helping cut losses in 1990 when the company was encountering difficulties. Although Cowie was not resident in the early stages of the negotiations, by moving to Maputo he became the major representative of the company in the Committee. He communicated regularly with the home office. He first sent daily and then weekly reports back to headquarters. A part of that communication was bound together in a wonderful "Notes from the High Commissioner's Desk," which we got a glimpse of. The reports that were included described humorously the problems he encountered in organizing personal and office life in Maputo, as well as the drier business aspects. But, in describing his personal experiences, he managed to make the documents communicate to headquarters a great deal about the business tasks at hand and his role as representative of the company.

He also won over the government side. One of the government team members described him as "friendly, understanding of the country, and very intelligent." Ceron said: "[Cowie] owns a project development personality. In my experience this is a special breed of person, part pioneer, part adventurer, part psychologist, and, above all, especially in [Cowie's] case, a complete leader with a focused objective. Many misunderstandings were avoided as a result of his attitudes that differed from those of some investors, whose approach may border on jingoism. He concentrated on making sure all players involved had real ownership of the project and their individual part in it, but always within the context of the Mozambican perspective. He developed what I call an 'us-ness' attitude as opposed to a 'they-us' situation. One last characteristic [Cowie] brought to the table: a firm belief in Mozambique and its people, that they could get the job done. This injected into his message a plausibility that motivated players to put their best efforts into the task at hand."

Cowie credited the Mozambique-born Isabel da Cruz, the second manager of the Mozambique Affairs Team, for playing a major role as his cultural "translator" in the negotiating process. Thus, the combination seemed especially effective.

Since these two managers were resident in Mozambique, they were always available for discussions with government. In fact, the importance of resident managers was underlined by an observer who described Cowie as being: "far from a long distance manager. In order to convey the level of commitment to both the MOZAL management and the Mozambican authorities, he was the first official actually to move his family into Maputo as a permanent resident. His family, in fact, was the 'test case' for debugging the delicate expatriate approval process."

Third, Minister Baloi, of the Ministry of Industry, Commerce, and Tourism, and other ministers on the Task Force provided the high-level support that was needed to strengthen the Committee. The support from the ministerial level enabled the core members of the Government Liaison Group to bring into their discussions representatives from other ministries and agencies whenever problems arose. As a result, they had considerable influence on other agencies and ministries to solve problems.

Fourth, when the issues were complicated, government officials and company managers learned to break into small working groups—the Task Groups—and meet with specialists to develop new ways of dealing with bureaucratic issues.

The next stage drew on these factors that had helped the company and the government to conclude the basic agreements.

5

Implementing the Agreement: A Serious Attack on Red Tape

Building a Continuing Structure

Implementation started even before the public announcement to go ahead was made in April 1998. As a result, new kinds of difficulties were already appearing. For example, the relocation of people from the construction site was moving along, but problems of compensation were constantly occurring. The location of access roads was proving difficult, partly because of uncertainties about the exact location of the toll road under construction. Both company managers and officials at the Investment Promotion Center were beginning to realize that some of the worst bureaucratic problems were coming in the implementation stage.

Even though these problems needed to be solved, attendance at the meetings of the Government Liaison Committee was falling off, with the finishing of the Investment Project Authorization. Its tasks appeared to be done. Company managers had begun meeting weekly at the Investment Promotion Center to deal with implementation problems. One of the results had already been the creation of a center for registering contractors for the construction stage. The group of company and government officials meeting to deal with these problems had even taken on a name, the IPA Working Team.

Yet, the informal meetings of the IPA Working Team did not seem adequate to the new challenges of implementation. Both sides recognized that a formal structure with high-level officials should continue to exist to deal with the looming problems of implementing the agreements that had been concluded. Thus, in late May they agreed to restructure the Government Liaison Committee and try to maintain the commitment of its members.

Over the next few months a revised structure emerged to ease implementation. This time, the structure would consist of three tiers. (See Figure 4.)

The Government Task Group

At the top tier of this revised structure, the Inter-ministerial Task Force would continue, but it was re-named as the Government Task Group (GTG). This group of ministers was still to be chaired by Baloi, the Minister of Industry, Commerce, and Tourism. Baloi would meet quarterly with Barbour, Mozal's chairman.

The IPA Steering Committee

A second tier, similar to the old one, would be continued. The old Government Liaison Committee would turn into the IPA Steering Committee. The core government team in this group should continue to reflect the make-up of the minister-level Government Task Group: representatives from the Ministry of Industry, Commerce and Tourism, the Ministry of Planning and Finance, the Ministry of Public Works and Housing, the Ministry of Environmental Affairs, and the Investment Promotion Center. The structure would, however, be flexible enough to include representatives of the Ministry of Labor, Customs, and other agencies important to implementing the project, when needed. The company team for this Committee would comprise five managers, with four alternates. The IPA Steer-

FIGURE 2
Coordinating Structure for Implementation

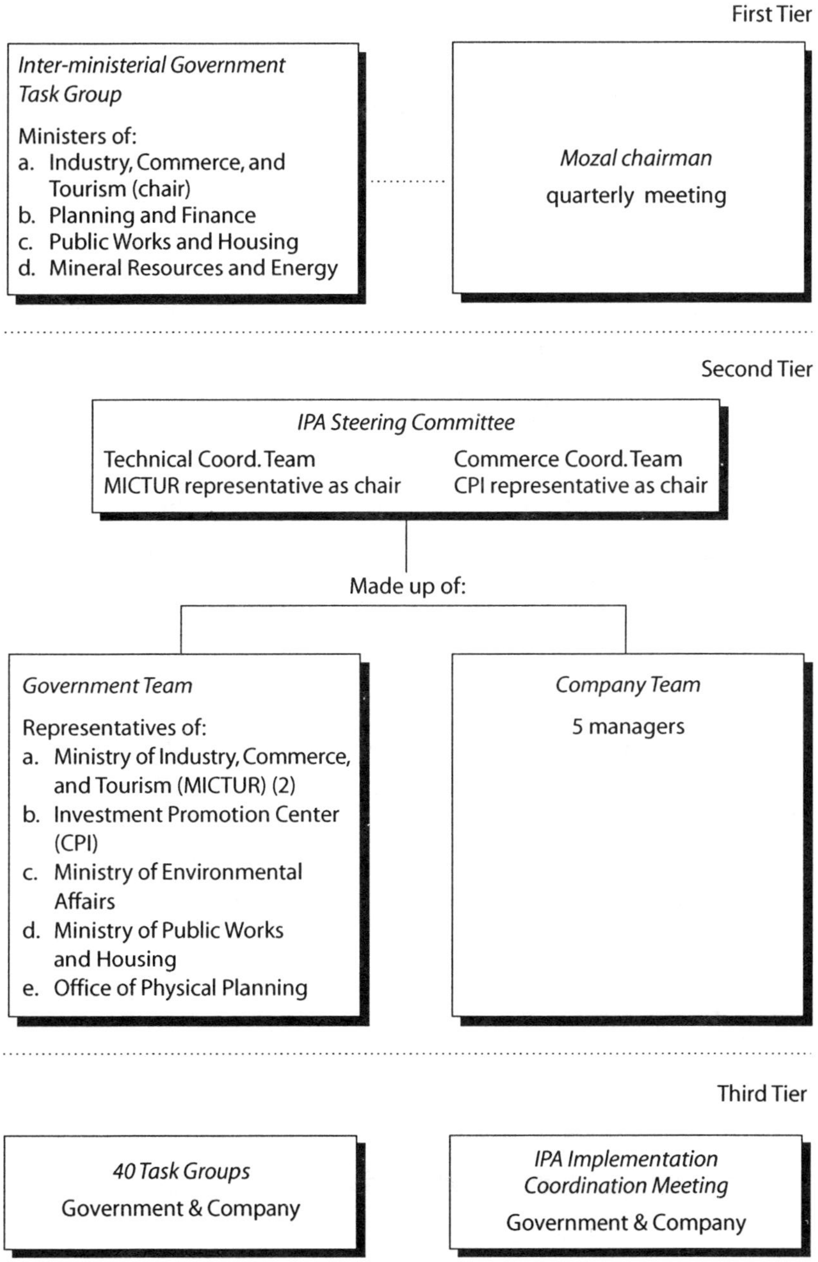

First Tier

Inter-ministerial Government Task Group

Ministers of:
a. Industry, Commerce, and Tourism (chair)
b. Planning and Finance
c. Public Works and Housing
d. Mineral Resources and Energy

Mozal chairman
quarterly meeting

Second Tier

IPA Steering Committee

Technical Coord. Team
MICTUR representative as chair

Commerce Coord. Team
CPI representative as chair

Made up of:

Government Team

Representatives of:
a. Ministry of Industry, Commerce, and Tourism (MICTUR) (2)
b. Investment Promotion Center (CPI)
c. Ministry of Environmental Affairs
d. Ministry of Public Works and Housing
e. Office of Physical Planning

Company Team

5 managers

Third Tier

40 Task Groups
Government & Company

IPA Implementation Coordination Meeting
Government & Company

ing Committee would be divided into two teams, the Technical Coordination Team (headed by S. Macamo[51] from the Ministry of Industry, Commerce, and Tourism) and the Commercial Coordination Team (headed by Dombo from the Investment Promotion Center). The Committee, which started meeting in April 1998, would meet once a month; the teams, weekly.

Increasing the Committee's influence, the Economic Council (a subgroup of the Council of Ministers) gave it formal approval and assigned its terms of reference:

1. To obtain feedback from the Technical and Commercial Coordination teams on progress made and to identify issues requiring higher level intervention.

2. To expedite resolution of critical issues.

3. To set guidelines and principles to be applied by task groups.

4. To identify critical issues impacting on [sic] project schedule and budget, and to agree on how to communicate these issues to the Government Task Group (GTG).

5. To provide regular communications to the GTG to ensure that key Ministers are kept fully informed on the project.

As pointed out, the make-up of the IPA Steering Committee was flexible; members were added or subtracted as needed. As of April 1999, for example, the Committee comprised six permanent members from the central government: from MICTUR (Mbeve and Macamo), CPI (Dombo), Office of Physical Planning (MPF) (A. Tivane), the Ministry for Environmental Action (F. Conte), and the Ministry of Public Works and Housing (V. Joaquim). For a meeting that month (April 29), minutes indicate that 12 government people were invited; they included six non-permanent members whose interests were affected by items to be discussed, or who had special skills relevant to the agenda. Some of these invitees were from organizations with permanent representation; others, from Customs, for example, were not.

The Task Groups

A new formal third tier was added to the structure for implementation. The Task Groups became formalized. The ones that existed as of August represented the agreements unfinished as of that date and the areas where government relations were expected to be important in implementing the agreement: Framework Plan, Land Concession, Road-Access to Site, Work Permits/Visas, TdM Telecommunications, Training, Drawings Approval, Electricity-EdM Construction Power Supply, Engineering Standards, Harbor: Maputo, Harbor: Matola, Land Mines, Registration of Contractors, Registration of Engineers, Relocation Program, Roads: Border to Matola, Roads: Harbor Link, Roads: N4 Toll, Sewerage Treatment Plant, Transportation of Mozambican Labor, and four teams for the various water arrangements. Later, other Task Groups were to be created as problems arose: for example, Environment Management Plan and Customs. Eventually as many as 40 Task Groups were formed. They were coordinated by the relevant Coordinating Team of the IPA Steering Committee.

Task Groups tried to solve difficult nitty-gritty problems before they rose higher in the structure. Consider the problem of getting contractors registered. Without help, it appeared that contractors would have to go from ministry to ministry to collect all the required permits and official stamps. This process could take each contractor up to six months, if the contractors had to do all this in the usual ways. The Task Group assembled a team from the Maputo Province comprising representatives of each office that had a role in the registration process. The team agreed to have someone from each office at the construction site every Tuesday. It became clear, however, that officials were reluctant to stamp approvals immediately at the site. Thus, it was agreed that representatives from the Investment Promotion Center would manage the following process: contractors would collect the required blank forms on one Tuesday; the next Tuesday they would bring the filled-out forms;

and on the third Tuesday, they would return and collect all the approved documents. The officials could use the week to complete and stamp the approvals in their own offices. The result was that a six-month process was reduced to two weeks, and a model for future investors had been established.

Sometimes the Task Groups established structures at the task level that more or less replicated the overall structure. For example, for the continuing negotiations concerning the port, there were monthly meetings of the Managing Director of Mozal with the chairman of the port and rail company. The Task Group had more frequent meetings, made up of a manager representing the port and rail company (CFM) and a manager from Mozal. As construction at the port began, the project manager for Mozal met weekly with the principal CFM engineer. And the CFM staff at the port site met daily with contractors.

The IPA Implementation Coordination Meeting at CPI

At the third tier, the Task Groups would be supplemented by a formal version of the IPA Working Team, which had already emerged as an informal organization. Renamed as the IPA Implementation Coordination Meeting, its members would gather weekly at the CPI. Difficulties unsolved by the Task Groups typically came first to this weekly meeting for resolution. Problems that could not be solved at this level went to the monthly meeting of the IPA Steering Committee.

Local Government

As implementation proceeded, the role of local government grew more important. The Maputo Province government was responsible for the resettlement program, informal trading in the area, police services, land issues, and various community concerns. As a result, a parallel structure was set up to bring local officials together with Mozal managers. The Technical Coordinating Team of the

IPA Steering Committee dealt directly with the provincial government, especially on infrastructure, resettlement, and liaison with community leaders. Moreover, the governor of Maputo Province (S. Nhaca) received copies of the minutes of all IPA Steering Committee meetings and met regularly with Minister Baloi, or the Government Task Group if necessary. Company management credited the province's governor with playing a key role in implementation.

Linkage Program

One more piece was added to the implementation structure. An important goal of both the company and the government was to involve local suppliers and contractors as early as possible in the construction of the smelter. To encourage this, a Linkage Program was created.[52] The guiding body, the Linkage Team, was created at the Investment Promotion Center. It comprised five people: one from the Ministry of Public Works, one from the Ministry of Industry, Commerce, and Tourism, and three from the Investment Promotion Center. The promotion center provided financial incentives, out of funds obtained from the World Bank, to encourage the participation of officials from outside the organization.[53] Since the company had established a Linkage Program at Richard's Bay, the team visited the company's other smelters and took potential contractors to see the activities of South African suppliers there. The visits enabled the Linkage Team members to identify opportunities for Mozambican firms and to search for companies in Mozambique that might accomplish what South African suppliers had done. The Team would visit potential local suppliers and ask whether they could provide the item or service needed. Mozal would help the Mozambican firms to obtain equipment and technical skills, and finance, and it would assist them in the preparation of bidding documents.

The Mozal Linkage Program came to be run out of the new Project Facilitation Center, which was established near the construction site, at Mozal's offices. The Investment Promotion Center assigned two people to this office.

Although a great deal of help had to be supplied to local firms before they could complete the bidding process and meet quality standards, the program was viewed as successful. More than $74 million of contracts had been signed with local firms by March 1999.[54] Moreover, as a result of the experience, the Investment Promotion Center established a permanent Linkage Division in its organization, with the goal of building linkages between local firms and other foreign investors in the future.

The Structure in Action

Task Groups tried to solve problems without having to refer them to the IPA Steering Committee. In fact, many problems could be dealt with at that tier, often through the help of officials from the Investment Promotion Center. An example was the difficulty the company was facing in obtaining expatriates' work permits. The Investment Promotion Center arranged meetings with the Ministry of Labor to solve the problem. Since the meeting was called by senior officials with clout, it put pressure on Labor officials to come up with solutions, and the pressure worked. It was hoped that the solutions developed in this case would be applied to expatriates needed in subsequent projects.

Some problems could not be solved at the third tier. Examples of issues that had to be sent up to the IPA Steering Committee were the need to expedite the registration of the new power company, the search for land for expatriate housing, and the determination of responsibility for harbor dredging. The IPA Steering Committee was important in dealing with procedures for exempting the company from the newly introduced value-added tax, as well. These issues all required the attention of high-level government officials and the kind of subtle pressure that the IPA Steering Committee could exert. But, on occasion, the Committee was also needed to resolve more mundane-seeming problems: for example, disputes about the quality of locally available cement and the need to establish procedures in the Ministry of Planning and Finance for the handling of temporary imports of vehicles.

It was not only the company that brought concerns to the various implementation groups. The regular meetings at each tier provided opportunities for government agencies to raise problems that they were encountering because of the project. Thus, one important issue to come before the group was allegations of smuggling. Customs noted that the reported imports of construction materials coming from South Africa through the principal road clearance point dropped to close to zero as Mozal's duty-free materials began to arrive. Customs assumed that the duty-free import of construction materials for the Mozal project was leading to smuggling—that importers were registering their construction material for other projects as being for Mozal.[55] The IPA Steering Committee provided a forum to discuss the problem. Since by this time the Committee had as a member an official from the Customs office, he knew the company managers and could comfortably bring the matter up with counterparts at Mozal. The goal was first to gather facts and then, if abuses were occurring, to seek ways of stopping them without imposing burdensome bureaucratic procedures. In the absence of the mechanism, it is likely that Customs would have simply raised administrative barriers, slowing the import of Mozal's material. As it was, a new set of procedures was worked out that satisfied both parties.

Environmental impact was an important concern of the government. Impact studies were required of the company and standards were developed. Still, worries grew as officials in the relevant ministry recognized that they did not have the funds to do an adequate job of monitoring the impact of Mozal's activities. These concerns could have led to burdensome rules, in the absence of some forum for reasoned discussion. But officials from the responsible ministry were able to work with Mozal managers through the liaison structures to understand the company's testing procedures. Once they were satisfied that they were adequate, ministry officials agreed to accept company data and to require only occasional spot checks of their accuracy.

The structure for solving problems during implementation seemed to work for both the company and the government. Perhaps the best indicator was that construction was ahead of schedule in June 1999, and plans were firm to begin commercial deliveries of aluminum in 2001.

6

What Was Accomplished?

When we conducted interviews in June 1999, most government officials and business managers in Mozambique concluded that the case-based approach for Mozal had been very successful; yet, some observers raised a few concerns.

The impact of the approach ought to be measured against two basic questions: First, how did the process affect the Mozal project. That is, did it speed up negotiations and implementation for this mega-project and did it result in a better deal for the country than might otherwise have been struck? Second, did the experience with Mozal result in a better investment climate for future investors?

The Impact on Mozal

Negotiation

The final version of the Heads of Agreement for the Mozal project was completed in less than six months after the two-tier negotiating structure was created. The Investment Project Authorization was concluded some nine months after the Heads of Agreement was signed. And many other problems were solved simultaneously. This is a respectably short time for the negotiation of such a huge and complex project in any country, but it is more impressive given the past performance of Mozambique in other difficult negotiations. The efforts to negotiate arrangements for the gas fields in the north of the country, for example, had begun before the Mozal project, but there was still no final agreement by June 1999. Although there are other explanations for delays in that particular project, the experience still suggests that negotiating "ministry-by-ministry" can lead to interminable negotiations.

The first tier of the negotiating structure, the Inter-ministerial Task Force, did indeed provide a shield against a danger inherent in the "ministry-by-ministry" approach to negotiations.[56] It contributed oversight that made sure that any barriers posed by one ministry or agency could be reviewed in light of the broad interests of the country, and that concessions by one ministry would be considered in the context of the whole agreement. But the formal Inter-ministerial Task Force would not alone have been sufficient to move the negotiations along. As busy as they were, ministers could not pay the kind of attention and master the details that were needed to push this complex project. The creation of the second tier, the Government Liaison Committee, dealt with this problem. Although very busy themselves, the members of the second-tier groups could devote the time and attention required to reach agreement. Important, they were high enough and sufficiently respected in their organizations to have access to their ministers and to influence bureaucrats in their own and other government units. The combination of the two tiers led to reasonable speed and to coordination among ministries.

Implementation and Monitoring

During the implementation process, what became a three-tier structure replicated the advantages of the two-tier structure to overcome bureaucratic barriers as they were encountered. The negotiating process had helped to create a group of officials who were committed to seeing the project through. The revised structure recaptured their attention and assured continuity of personnel. When the company encountered problems, managers turned to individuals in ministries and agencies who had been involved all along, with whom trust had been built, and who had the influence needed to solve problems. Issues were tackled first at low levels, and then passed up to the higher levels in the structure if they could not be solved at a lower tier.

The contacts and trust that were built in the efforts to solve the company's problems also turned out to be valuable when the government saw problems. Too often, when officials and managers have not established relationships, officials to try to solve problems on their own. The result is easily more bureaucratic red tape and a delay in implementing projects. The story reported earlier about suspected smuggling provides one illustration of the importance of relationships in creating solutions to perceived problems without increasing red tape.

Moreover, in many cases countries have no on-going mechanism to ensure that foreign investors honor the conditions of the agreements they enter. Rather unexpectedly, the arrangements built during the implementation stage encouraged the development of reasonable ways for the government to enforce the terms of the agreement. In fact, the on-going negotiating and implementation structures provided a degree of monitoring that had been absent in other projects in Mozambique. This occurred particularly through the regular on-site presence of government members of the Task Groups. The environmental issues, discussed earlier, illustrate one solution to monitoring problems. Housing provided another example. As housing was being built for former residents displaced by the project, members of the Task Groups raised questions about whether the required standards were being met. They believed that housing should be of a higher standard and that the company should assure title to adequate farmland for farmers displaced by the project. Discussions were held in the IPA Implementation Committee meetings, and plans were redesigned to meet government expectations.

The Overall Agreement

It is difficult to know whether the approach in this case resulted in a basic agreement that was more favorable to the country than what would have emerged from some other approach. A few bilateral and multilateral donors to Mozambique have criticized the tax arrangements for Mozal, arguing that they undermine efforts to increase government revenue. There is, however, no evidence that the government would have negotiated a more favorable agreement under a different approach. In this case, officials knew why they were agreeing to the fiscal regime offered Mozal. They believed that the investor saw the project as being very risky and that the company needed correspondingly large incentives. They also believed that attracting a huge project and getting it into operation quickly would bring other investors to the country. This potential externality was extremely important to officials. Finally, the existing Industrial Free Zone legislation authorized these, and more, benefits. No matter what the negotiating structure, negotiators would probably have found it difficult to deny benefits for which the "pioneer" company appeared to be eligible under legislation already in place. In fact, in requiring the company to pay taxes after only one year of production, the government gave the company less than it could have under the Industrial Free Zone legislation.[57]

Even those development assistance organizations that accept the wisdom of the terms granted Mozal have expressed worries that the government would be compelled by the precedent to offer subsequent investors incentives similar to those given Mozal, even if those subsequent investors do not have the same "pioneer" characteristics. On the other hand, government officials did believe that Mozal was a special case, as the first investor in a mega-project, and that subsequent investors would face a more certain environment. Thus, officials argued to us that the success of this project would mean that the government would not need to offer later investors such sweeteners to attract them to the country. The worry remains, however, since many other governments have indeed found it difficult to withhold from later investors the same favorable terms that were granted earlier entrants.

Fears have also been expressed that the agreement will not last, and that eventual renegotiations will damage the country's image among investors. Experience elsewhere suggests the possibility that the government will forget the special circumstances of a "pioneer" investor, if the project turns out to be very profitable. Terms that seemed reasonable at the outset can eventually appear unfairly to favor the company. In that event, negotiations may be re-opened in order to capture more of the returns for the country.[58] On the other hand, events could well go the other way. If, for example, prices of aluminum continue to fall, and the project thus turns out to be unprofitable, the company may well ask for relief from the tax on turnover.[59] After all, under the free-zone arrangements, Mozal has to pay the one percent tax even if the project is losing money, unlike under an income tax where no profits mean no tax.

Stability in investment agreements is desirable, but often elusive. It is unlikely that another approach to negotiation would have increased the prospects for stability. One can be reasonably sure only that the liaison approach used to conclude the Mozal agreement allowed government officials to weigh the whole package of terms in light of the circumstances and beliefs at the time of the negotiations. That is probably all one can ask for.

The Impact on Future Investors

A Model for Negotiating Mega-Projects

Potential investors in other mega-projects have viewed the government's approach to the Mozal negotiations as offering a way for them to assemble the kinds of agreements and permits that would be almost impossible to gather in a reasonable time under the old approaches. According to company managers, Minister Baloi has told prospective new investors: "Mozal is the model that will be used for every [mega-] project that will happen in this country." On the table was Enron's proposed gas-related Maputo Iron and Steel Project (MISP). Indeed, Enron managers had been told directly by the government to turn to Mozal for a model of how it should proceed. In response, some Enron managers sat in on a few meetings of the Mozal IPA Steering Committee to see how it worked. In spring 1999, proposals for two additional mega-projects were advancing: a Sasol petrochemical plant, at Beira, and another aluminum smelter (by Fluor-Daniel and Kaiser), also at Beira. Both these "mega-projects" raised the kinds of problems that the liaison structure had been able to solve in the case of Mozal.

The model projected for negotiating these investments included the same two-tier concept: a Task Force of ministers, chaired by the sector minister, to oversee and support the negotiation process and a powerful Government Liaison Committee, made up of high-level trusted professionals of the affected ministries and agencies.[60] The Investment Promotion Center would play an important role in moving the projects along.

If some of the same officials who worked on Mozal could be involved in the new negotiations, then learning from the Mozal experience could be institutionalized and utilized for more projects. In fact, preparations for capturing the experience were well underway in 1999. The Investment Promotion Center, for example, had begun explicitly to view Mozal meetings as a training ground for its officials. One person being trained this way was scheduled to become the CPI representative for future negotiations on the proposed steel project.

Yet, the approach was very human-capital intensive in a country with an extreme shortage of skilled bureaucrats. While the government was capable of working with Mozal on a very close basis, it would be difficult to work with more than one or two such investors at the same time. While this may not seem like too great a problem, it must be remembered that the Mozal process will have taken more than five years, from the first meeting of the investor with the Government until planned first commercial production.

Moreover, there are some risks associated with too closely repeating the Mozal approach. If the same people are involved, the government might find it difficult to take a fresh look at problems that appear on the surface to be similar to those of Mozal, but which are, in fact, different. A U.S. investor in an aluminum smelter, for example, might face a different tax system at home from that faced by a South African investor. Thus, under some circumstances a U.S. company would strongly prefer an income tax to Mozal's turnover tax. It is possible that a different form of taxation would mean more revenue for the Mozambique government *and* for the U.S. company. However, as long as a negotiating team is not locked into its precedents, it can explore alternatives.

This potential problem appears to be manageable. Mozambique's experience with production sharing agreements for petroleum provides grounds for optimism. When it negotiated a gas agreement with ARCO, a U.S. company, the government brought in foreign consultants to help with adapting its past agreements to U.S. tax rules. As a result, the tax provisions for the American company were structured differently and both the government and the company probably gained from the flexibility.

It may not be easy for a cross-ministerial team such as the Government Liaison Group to work well with foreign consultants on technical issues. But, if the Investment Promotion Center or the tutelary ministry contract with experts and the experts then work closely with the relevant specialists on the team, then the requisite flexibility may be forthcoming. It appears to us that the gains from reproducing the approach outweigh this kind of risk.

Benefits for both Mega-Projects and Smaller Projects

Although the government was likely to replicate the multi-tiered liaison structure for mega-projects, it was not going to do so for small and medium projects. The costs in terms of time of both government officials and company managers would be too great. If investors in small projects gain from the Mozal experience, the benefits would have to be found elsewhere. We, and a number of other observers, believe that the Mozal case-based approach did indeed make permanent changes that will benefit subsequent investments, both large and small.

This study has pointed out several examples where the liaison groups for Mozal reduced bureaucratic problems, making lasting improvements as changes in customs clearance illustrate. Mozal managers claimed that new procedures reduced the time required for customs clearance from three to six weeks to 24 hours. This change came only as the result of much joint work. After long, frustrating, and unsuccessful efforts to reduce clearance time, managers issued a challenge: "get clearance down to 24 hours or there's no project." Although it took three more days of negotiations to design a system that would satisfy the 24-hour rule, a system did emerge. And when smuggling was alleged through the clearance arrangements for Mozal's duty-free goods Customs and the company were able to sit down together and modify the system to maintain the goal of quick clearance and still provide security. By spring 1999, the import procedures built for Mozal were said to have resulted in accelerated clearance for all importers, cutting time by at least 50 percent. In another case described earlier, the Mozal negotiations clarified matters for future investors. At the time the Mozal Investment Project Authorization was signed, Mozambique did not have a value-added tax. The IPA exempted the company from the existing sales tax and from any similar taxes. Although this provision would seem to cover the value-added tax introduced in 1999, bureaucrats in the tax office were hesitant to issue a clear statement that the company is exempt from the new tax. Rather than having to go to the minister, the company brought the issue to the IPA Steering Committee. With the resulting pressure from the Committee to resolve the matter, the tax office quickly confirmed that the company was not subject to the new value-added tax. The ruling would, presumably, set a precedent for any future investor in similar circumstances.

In addition, the Mozal process provided models for solving some frustrating bureaucratic problems. One important example, described earlier, was the system built for speeding the registration of contractors. Having been proved, this system could be copied by other investors. Similarly, before Mozal, the Ministry of Labor approved work permits for expatriates on a case-by-case method. The process could be long and the results unpredictable. For Mozal, the Ministry of Labor agreed to accept a list of expatriates and review the list as a whole. The result was more rapid processing and less paper work. Moreover, the list was consistently approved. Having once followed the procedure, the Ministry was likely to agree to a similar process for subsequent investors, even though the Mozal procedures had not become standard practice.

Similarly to the work permit (and visa) issues, telephone installation time for Mozal was dropped to 48 hours. According to Cowie, the task in such examples was to show the agencies that "they *can* do it. Then they can do it *again*."

The most important impact of the Mozal negotiations on future investors was probably the creation of a cadre of government officials from different agencies and ministries who had gained a good deal of knowledge of the problems that foreign investors (and domestic investors, for that matter) face in setting up businesses in Mozambique. The Mozal experience built a pro-investment attitude and a problem-solving mentality in the government officials involved. By the spring of 1999 there were, in each relevant ministry, officials who knew exactly what kinds of problems investors face, how those problems affect investment, and which ministries, agencies, and individuals held the keys to solving the problems. The building of this cadre served several functions:

1. Direct help to investors: Not only Mozal, but other investors as well, learned that the officials involved with Mozal were the people who were likely to understand their problems and be able to help resolve them.

One of the most frustrating experiences of business managers operating in emerging markets is the difficulty of knowing whom to contact when problems arise. Or, in getting officials, once contacted, to take some personal responsibility in helping them solve problems. Many are the stories of unanswered phone calls when officials do not want to take decisions with regard to investor problems. By mid-1999, foreign investors already in Mozambique knew whom to call in each ministry or agency (in the central or provincial government) when they needed questions answered or solutions to problems: officials who had served as members of the Government Liaison Committee, the IPA Steering Committee, or one of the Task Groups for Mozal.

2. Help by the CPI: The Mozambican investment promotion agency (CPI) saw one of its principal tasks as assisting new foreign investors to obtain the permits, approvals, and actions they need from the various government ministries and agencies. In a bureaucracy that had a reputation for being slow in responding to requests and for not having a problem-solving attitude, it was especially important that new investors could find help in this process. To provide effective assistance, CPI officials needed to be able to identify individuals in each agency or ministry who had the authority to issue the required permits and approvals and to resolve problems quickly. In fact, service would be much better if CPI officials and those in the relevant ministries and agencies really knew each other well. CPI officials said that the experience of working jointly with individuals from other ministries and agencies on the Mozal case had reinforced for them the kinds of relationships that they needed so that they could help future investors. This seemed to be true.

3. Leadership in changing legislation, procedures, etc: Participation in the Mozal process changed officials' attitudes. The role of government became clearer to some officials. One, for example, said that the Mozal exposure had convinced him that the government cannot leave investors to struggle with land issues. The government itself had to deal effectively with compensation and avoidance of land speculation. More broadly, an official said that the experience had "built a culture of collecting necessary information and looking at practice in other countries." The experience of the cadre of officials involved with Mozal negotiations also led their own ministers to have more confidence in them. As a result their recommendations on removing bureaucratic barriers were particularly likely to receive favorable attention.

Officials with experience in the Mozal case, for example, made recommendations for revisions in the new Industrial Free Zone legislation that was working its way through the legislative process at the time of our interviews. The changes were to correct flaws and omissions identified in this experience. More generally, one government official noted that the Mozal experience led officials to pay a lot more attention to who was responsible for what in this and all subsequent legislation that affected investment.

Especially important was the support the experience gave to the Investment Promotion Center (CPI) in one of its most important functions, improving the investment climate in Mozambique.[61] Since its officials, along with those from the Ministry of Industry, Commerce, and Tourism, were among the most active in the negotiation and implementation process for Mozal, they had gained a great deal of expertise about problems investors face. Knowing the problems and being associated with this highly visible project helped build the reputation of CPI. The resulting knowledge and prestige placed CPI officials in a stronger position to press for changes in laws, regulations, and procedures that would improve the overall investment climate in Mozambique.

The experience was also eventually to elevate the influence of several individual members of the Government Liaison Group, enabling them to exert more effective pressure within the government for reform. As the final version of this paper was being prepared, the authors received notice that Sumbana, the director of the Investment Promotion Center, had been promoted to Minister of Tourism,[62] and had joined the Council of Ministers. His new position and his experience in the successful Mozal negotiations should enable him to be even more effective in the on-going attacks on red tape and other barriers to investment.

4. *Provincial and municipal government and other investors as allies:* In some countries, provincial and municipal governments create barriers to foreign investors. Often officials do not fully understand the impact of the barriers they raise. By involving local government in the discussions at the implementation stage, Mozambique managed to educate a set of officials at this level on the adverse impact of red tape on investment in their region. Some of the solutions worked out for local government issues were available for subsequent investors.

The linkage program also created allies for foreign investment outside government. Local investors often see foreign investors as interlopers. According to one official, Mozambique "used to have newspaper articles saying that foreign companies took opportunities [from local firms]. Now, no more. [Local firms] see foreign investors as opportunities." Suspicions of foreign investors had certainly not disappeared, but such investors seemed more welcome than in the past.

In summary, the innovative program for the Mozal smelter project was credited by both the private sector and the government in Mozambique with improving the investment climate in the country. Interviewees were quite adamant in their belief that the rapid negotiations and the smoothness of implementation improved Mozambique's reputation abroad. As one interviewee put it, "It is very helpful to Mozambique when Billiton's managers have lunch with business people in London and say good things about doing business in Mozambique." In fact, *The Africa Competitiveness Report,* cited at the beginning of this study, contains some evidence of investors' changing perceptions. In spite of the low ranking it gave Mozambique on a number of measures of investment climate, it placed the country fourth from the top on "improvement (1992–1997)." Moreover, Mozambique appeared at the very top on the "optimism index (1997–1999)," which seemed to reflect investors' views of the country's prospects.[63] But, a better reputation alone does not increase investment; it only encourages potential investors to take a look at the country. In the end, they have to see some real change in the investment climate. By 1999, change did, in fact, seem to have resulted. Equally important, when this study was being conducted there was a strong belief on the part of both the government officials and private sector business people that not all the positive effects of the program had been felt: problems facing the investor in the implementation stage were still being solved, and new attitudes on the part of government officials were continuing to affect legislation and procedures that governed both domestic and foreign investment in Mozambique.

7

Reproducing the Case-based Approach

O ther countries can, we believe, copy the Mozal case-based approach and have similar successes in encouraging bureaucratic reform. Moreover, they might do even better, by adopting some suggestions made by officials who participated in the program in Mozambique.

What Are the Essential Characteristics?

If a country is to replicate the Mozal process, it must identify the aspects of the experience that were essential to success. We believe that the following actions should be taken if similar results are to be obtained:

1. *Build commitment on the part of officials to reform:* Members of the Government Liaison Group for Mozal had a deep commitment to reforming the bureaucratic process. For most, this commitment had been built in the earlier steps of Mozambique's war on red tape. Officials from the Investment Promotion Center had, for example, played significant roles in the first step of attacking red

tape, the private sector conferences. Since the Center saw improving the investment climate as its priority in attracting foreign investment, its members were especially determined to use the Mozal project to effect reform. Minister Baloi had also been involved in the private sector conferences and was chairman of the Inter-ministerial Working Group to Remove Administrative Barriers to Investment, which had been organized in the second step in the battle against red tape. Although the aluminum smelter fell within the sectors to be supported by his ministry, his broader interest in reducing investment barriers added to his own backing of the Committees and to the commitment and role of his ministry's representatives in the process.

In the heat of negotiations the goal of reducing bureaucratic red tape for future investors was often forgotten. But these individuals were so committed to the broader issue of helping future investors that they frequently returned to this important task.

Both the commitment and the resulting pressure from higher levels showed up in the attendance record of officials in the discussions. Consider only a few examples: In the six meetings of the Government Liaison Committee for which we had attendance records, the two principal representatives of the Ministry of Industry, Commerce, and Tourism (Mbeve and Moyane) were present in five. The representatives of the port and rail company (Bainha) and the Ministry of Public Works and Housing (Joaquim) had perfect attendance records for the meetings to which they were invited. For the Implementation Steering Committee, we had records for 28 meetings. The CPI's Dombo or Tivane, or both, attended 24 of these meetings. From the Ministry of Industry, Commerce, and Tourism, Macamo was present 74% of the time. These are strikingly good records.

Observers pointed out that this kind of attendance record was not necessarily to be expected from government officials in Mozambique. Several of the officials on the Committee had had little experience dealing with foreigners and most of that had been with development assistance officials, as opposed to businesspeople.

As a result of this and their lack of knowledge of the engineering issues, some Committee members seemed rather intimidated at the outset. But, they attended meetings anyway, and soon developed the necessary self-confidence. Moreover, because of problems in attracting busy officials to similar out-of-office meetings, a pattern was developing in the country that officials were paid extra to attend meetings. The World Bank, for example, was paying $50 each for certain meetings, according to one member of the Committee. But, both ministers and company managers preferred to have attendance based on commitment to the project and to reform. One company manager said he reminded officials when they slacked off: "Mr. Baloi wants answers. It's in your interest to attend."

2. *Select one important and appropriate investment project:* The liaison experiment dealt with only one investment project. This is the core of the case-based approach. One could imagine an initial effort that assigned several projects to a liaison group, but we believe that the resulting dilution of attention would have led to a much less effective undertaking. Thus we are convinced that it is essential to start with a single project.

The importance of the project meant that it had captured wide attention in Mozambique. The prime minister of Mozambique had expressed his strong support for the Mozal project. He visited the Richard's Bay smelter early and made positive public statements about the implications of the investment for Mozambique and the need to make it happen. Typical of his support, we were told, were the prime minister's comments to Customs: "If Mozal fails, Mozambique fails." This attitude put pressure on the various parties to move toward agreement and to solve problems quickly in the implementation stage. If the negotiations or implementation had failed, the responsible officials would certainly have had a lot of explaining to do to the prime minister. We believe that the chances of success would have been much smaller absent this kind of support.

Importance also matters on the company side. The size of Mozal and its importance to company strategy made it worthwhile for the sponsoring company to station in Mozambique, from early on, resident managers with authority to carry on discussions and to make important decisions with regard to the proposed investment.

The company chosen must be one that is willing to send managers who will cooperate with officials at various levels, not only in solving its problems but in trying to pave the way for subsequent investors. Government officials we interviewed described the Mozal managers as having a "very positive attitude" and being "friendly." They were said to "try to understand" the government's problems and concerns, "as young people who could accept new ideas."

Certainly not essential, but helpful, was the fact that the sponsor of the Mozal project had a similar plant in a neighboring country. Consequently, it was possible to hold meetings at a plant almost identical to the one being constructed in Mozambique, giving life to managers' attitudes of "you can have a similar facility." Although proximity probably helped in building the linkage program as well, having a similar plant so close is not likely to be an option for most countries, and is not essential to success.

3. *Discourage direct negotiation at the top of government:* As important as it was for top levels of government to support the project, it was equally important that the president and the prime minister avoided direct intervention in the negotiation process. There was never a direct or indirect signal to company managers that they could do better by negotiating directly with higher authorities to solve problems. By holding to this attitude, the president and the prime minister gave the responsibility as well as the authority to the formal groups to negotiate and solve problems as they arose.

This approach contrasts with that in some other countries. Presidents or prime ministers are too often willing to make decisions that undermine their negotiating teams. Their intent may be to speed up the process, but the outcome is often perverse. Company managers soon learn to take difficult problems over the heads of the groups assigned to negotiate, with quick demoralization of officials charged with negotiating or with solving problems.[64]

The company's attitude was, in this case, consistent with the government position. Multinationals differ in their attitudes and the ways in which they deal with governments.[65] Another company might have regularly short-circuited the liaison process and tried to go directly to the prime minister or the president to solve problems, rather than working through the sometimes slow bureaucracy.[66] Mozal's policy was clear: Do not go to higher levels to deal with problems that are assigned to a given level. Thus, managers worked hard to solve problems in the working teams.

The company's approach built respect within their ministries for the members of the teams, and eventually it strengthened the power of the appointed teams in settling issues. As they gained prestige, the members of the team were better able to use their new knowledge to improve the investment climate in Mozambique.

The combination of attitudes strengthened the process greatly.

4. *Build a multi-tiered structure:* The two-tiered structure created for the Mozal negotiations involved officials from the ministerial level (at the Inter-ministerial Task Force) to the national director level (in the Government Liaison Committee and eventually the IPA Implementation Committee). In the implementation stage, the third tier (the Task Groups and the IPA Implementation Coordination Meetings) was added to include officials who actually implemented rules and regulations. Each tier played an important role.

a. As this study has pointed out, the Task Force at the ministerial level was important for several reasons: First, binding decisions on the basic agreement could be taken only with the consent of the Council of Ministers, key members of which were represented on the Task Force. Second, major differences in views across agencies could be resolved only at this level. Third, the deep involvement of officials at the ministerial level put pressure on the officials at the second level to perform well. The reports that Liaison Group members had to make to their ministers after Committee meetings served an educational role for ministers, who would face similar decisions in the future. Further, the reports put pressure on Liaison Group members to support their positions with sound arguments that could be defended to their ministers. Fourth, the regular participation of the ministers meant that they should have agreed to all the terms of the investment agreement by the time it was sent to them for approval. Finally, the Task Force created a group that could hold informed and effective discussions with the company chairman when very important issues had to be discussed at that level.

b. The Government Liaison Committee was necessary, as has been pointed out, because ministers could not afford the time to deal with all the issues that had to be negotiated and to do the kind of research required to learn about practices elsewhere. Further, the ministries needed to develop specialists on foreign direct investment at a level below the ministers; experience in the Liaison Group developed these skills.

c. Task Groups and the IPA Implementation Coordination Meetings at the CPI brought together the technical company managers and the bureaucrats who were responsible for procedures, rules, and so on that could create problems in implementation. In fact, many problems were resolved at this third tier.

5. Provide high-level government officials at the second-tier: The members of the Government Liaison Group and the IPA Steering Committee were at the National Director level. These are high level officials who were named by their ministers and had their confidence. As a result, their ministers almost always respected the positions taken by these senior officials. They grew to be true representatives of the ministers in the negotiations.

The confidence that ministers had in their representatives was to prove important later, as these same officials offered proposals for reform. The ministers grew to recognize these officials as the experts.

6. Allow flexible representation: The company and government members of the liaison group agreed that it was appropriate to invite to meetings any party who should have a role in the discussions of any item on the agenda. Thus when problems arose that required attention from ministries or agencies, national or local, officials from those organizations were invited to meetings to help solve problems.

7. *Formalize procedures:* Early on, a number of formalized procedures were developed. (See Chapter 3.) Meetings of all levels of the liaison process were held regularly, agendas were circulated in advance of meetings, written minutes were required of the liaison group after each meeting, and members of the Government Liaison Group were required to report after each meeting to their ministers. Each of these procedures played an important part in the success of the liaison approach.

a. Regular meetings: Meetings of the Government Liaison Committee were scheduled for designated Thursdays every month. Regularly scheduled monthly meetings continued with the IPA Steering Committee. The IPA Implementation Coordination Meetings were similarly scheduled for each week. Knowing the meeting dates far in advance removed excuses for absences. Further, the regular meetings enabled government officials to remain apprised of progress on the project, even if no issues were pressing. (It seems, however, that there was always some matter that needed to be discussed.).

b. Prepared agendas: The parties learned to prepare an agenda for circulation before each meeting. Although company managers actually prepared the agendas, they contacted government members of the Committee to ask for the top five items of concern to the government to combine with the top five issues of concern to the company. The agendas enabled members to consider issues before meetings. Government members could discuss their positions on the issues with their ministers, if they were likely to be controversial.

c. Written minutes: The company side prepared minutes after each meeting of the Government Liaison Committee and, later, the IPA Steering Committee. The minutes reported attendance (by name and organization), absentees (similarly by name and organization), and the items discussed in the meeting, with a brief summary of any conclusions reached. The minutes were circulated among the attendees for comments and to ensure that all interpretations of conclusions reached in the meeting were correct. After corrections, the minutes went to Minister Baloi, as Chairman of the Task Force (and thence, presumably, to members of the Task Force), to Barbour, the Chairman of Mozal's board, to I. Reid, the Managing Director of Mozal, and to members of the Government Liaison Committee. The minutes served to encourage attendance by government officials, since they informed ministers of who was present and who was absent. The brief reports on the meetings helped inform ministers of the discussions. And they preserved a record of resolved and unresolved issues.

d. Reports to ministers: Each government member of the Government Liaison Committee was required to provide a briefing to his or her minister after each meeting of the Committee. The briefings enabled the members to explain positions they had taken, make recommendations on still-unresolved issues, and receive instructions for the future. These briefings were either written or oral, depending on the preferences of the ministers and their delegates.

e. Language: The discussions in the various meetings were held in English; in fact, the foreign company managers did not speak Portuguese. But since not all the Mozambicans were completely confident in their ability in English, and language differences could create misunderstandings, a translator was available in meetings of the Government Liaison Committee and its successor IPA Steering Committee to deal with any language problems that might arise.

8. *Extend the process into the implementation stage:* The decision to extend the liaison structure into the implementation stage was very important. The process was originally designed to accelerate the conclusion of the Investment Project Authorization, but, as Cowie put it, "Company management initially thought that getting

the IPA was the problem. It soon discovered that the real problems would come during the implementation stage." Not only did the extension of the structure into the implementation stage help solve the "real problems," but it also gave government officials the kind of in-depth knowledge that they would need to solve problems for future investors.

9. Institutionalize the structures and capture the learning: The Mozambique government began to institutionalize the process before formal structures had been disbanded and lessons lost.[67] For example, the Inter-ministerial Task Force would continue to meet for other mega-projects. Only the chairmanship would differ, to reflect the different sectors that investment was to enter. As mentioned, during the Mozal negotiation and implementation, potential investors were sent by the government to meetings of the Government Liaison Committee or the Implementation Steering Committee to show them what they could anticipate. Thus, expectations of continuity were built.

Explicit training efforts also help in institutionalizing the experience. As mentioned, government "trainees" were brought to meetings of the Committees so that they could participate in similar groups in the future. As a result, junior members learned the process and could be moved on to higher positions in subsequent negotiations.

At the implementation level, the efforts to turn local firms into suppliers to Mozal led to the creation of a permanent Linkage Division in the Investment Promotion Center. This captured in-house the experience that had come from identifying and developing suppliers for the smelter.

Although not all decisions and procedures worked out at the implementation stage were documented and publicized (see below), the outlines of solutions to problems were widely known and could be reproduced when similar problems arose for subsequent investors.

Finally, by the time of this study, none of the government participants had been hired away by the private sector, as so often happens elsewhere. Pride in accomplishment and increased status must have been part of the incentive of these officials to remain in government. Their staying was an important element in capturing the learning from the Mozal experience. They could participate more effectively than inexperienced officials could in future arrangements, they could use their growing influence to help future investors through their problems, and they had gained stature that increased their influence within the government as champions of reform.[68]

Improving the Model

In our discussions, some people involved in the experiment made suggestions for improvements to make the case approach work better.

First, one government official who was important to the effort was disappointed that the Government Liaison Group never met as a group before the joint meetings of the Government Liaison Committee. He would have preferred to see some of the differences among the government representatives discussed and resolved in the absence of representatives from the other side. The resulting problems were most serious when new people were introduced to the process. On occasion, new members started with a belligerent stance, rather than a problem-solving attitude. He believed that having government officials meet before each Committee meeting would have helped acculturation of new members and resolution of differences of opinion, but he understood that time constraints were a major factor in keeping these meetings from taking place.

Second, several people said that the pressure to move ahead, especially in the implementation stage, meant that a number of the procedures developed to reduce red tape and speed up decision making had not been carefully documented. He believed that later investors would have benefited more if very careful write-ups had been produced of procedures that had been worked out, modified through experience, and proved successful. He would have preferred that these documents then be made public.

In a third suggestion for improvement, an official stated his disappointment that there was not enough overlap between personnel involved in the Mozal liaison effort and the "red-tape" commission established to serve the Inter-ministerial Working Group to Remove Administrative Barriers to Investment. The Working Group could have benefited from the detailed knowledge that officials accumulated during the Mozal effort. Although Minister Baloi and some of the members of the Government Coordinating Committee were involved in other steps of the program to reduce red tape,[69] perhaps more joint assignments would have been beneficial.

Fourth, the lack of any government budgetary support for the Government Liaison Group was criticized. The Group had no staff and no money from the government for research or travel, or for other expenses. Luckily, in this case the Investment Promotion Center did have access to some funds from the World Bank, a part of which it allocated to costs associated with the Government Liaison Group (GLG). For example, it provided funds for GLG members to travel to learn about experiences of other countries with free-trade zones. Mozal itself ended up funding and setting up offices for the CPI Project Team. This required some care on the part of both company and government to avoid any kind of image that the Investment Promotion Center had been "bought" by the company. The whole process might have worked more smoothly with some kind of government funding.

Finally, it was pointed out that any effort to reproduce the Mozal process elsewhere would have to take into account differences in government structure and regulations. For example, in some countries the core members of any Government Liaison Committee might need to incorporate a representative from the central bank, if foreign exchange regulations are especially difficult.

We believe that all these suggestions are good ones, worthy of consideration by any government that wants to follow a case-based approach to reducing bureaucratic barriers to investment.

A Program for Reducing Red Tape

Although managers and government officials concluded that the Mozal case-based approach benefited both this project and future investors, it is also important to keep in mind that the Mozal experiment was, in fact, part of a larger program to attack red tape in Mozambique. Other countries that are trying to reduce red tape ought to consider adopting all parts of the program, not just a single piece.

The program, the reader will remember from the first chapter, consisted of four steps, each of which played an important role in the attack on bureaucratic barriers to investment in Mozambique:

1. The first step had been the initiation of a series of private sector conferences. These conferences had successfully brought together business people and government people to discuss the barriers that faced investors in the country. They allowed the business community to express its concerns and priorities. The result was an increased awareness on the part of government officials of the problems the business community faced. More important, the conferences built political pressure for the government to act to reduce bureaucratic barriers to investment. And they constituted an annual "scoring event" by which the government was under pressure to produce results.

2. The second step was the production of a "catalog" of exactly what the barriers to investment were. Businesspeople's complaints tended to be a bit too vague to generate action. And businesspeople often overlooked the goals of regulations; as a result, they sometimes wanted to do away with regulations entirely, even though some had a purpose. Better was to offer solutions that would reduce the barriers but still accomplish relevant objectives. The study produced by FIAS provided the detailed list of exactly what the unnecessary barriers were; it was also sensitive to the need for the government to retain some regulation of certain areas.

3. The third step was the creation of the Inter-ministerial Working Group to Remove Administrative Barriers to Investment. The

high-level group pressed for reform and made some progress, especially in generating changes in legislation. It was less effective, however, at the level of nitty-gritty bureaucratic procedures.

4. The fourth step, and the principal subject of this study, was the case-based effort with Mozal, which was especially effective at the nitty-gritty level.

The various steps were complementary, and several individuals' roles spanned more than one part of the program. Almost certainly, the combination of steps was more effective than any single step alone.

Appendix 1
Mozambique: the Country

Mozambique, with a population of just under 18 million in 1996, stretches along the east coast of southern Africa. It borders on South Africa, Swaziland, Zimbabwe, Zambia, Malawi, and Tanzania. Its GDP of only US$123 per capita in 1998[70] ranked it among the lowest income countries in the world. Yet, the country was widely hailed for its recent change in development policies and the rapid growth rates that seemed to result from its economic reforms. It was viewed as a star in Africa by international institutions; it had been viewed somewhat less favorably by many foreign investors, not because of its policies, but because of the red tape that accompanied them. In the widely circulated report on competitiveness in Africa, Mozambique ranked 18th out of 23 African countries.[71] The low ranking was heavily influenced by the low ratings given to tax regulations and rates, regulations for starting business, uncertainty on costs of regulations, and other bureaucratic matters. While the international institutions focused on the success of the country in creating macro economic stability, investors reacted to the bureaucracy, where reforms had not yet taken hold.

From soon after its independence in 1975 from Portugal until 1992, the country had been engulfed in a civil war that was supported, for much of that time, by neighboring countries. At the outset, the Frelimo government pushed central planning, state ownership, and inward-looking development policies. The destruction wrought by the war and the socialist economic policies in the early years of independence led to a substantial decline in per capita GDP and a wrecked infrastructure.

In the mid-1980s, the Frelimo government turned away from central planning. The 1992 peace accords, combined with the new economic policies, set the stage for recovery. Democratic elections in 1994 confirmed Frelimo and its new policies. Reforms introduced included deregulation of prices, conservative fiscal and monetary policies, rationalized and lower tariffs (to an average rate of about 9% in 1999), and privatization of banks and a wide range of other previously state-owned businesses. Efforts were being made to restore infrastructure, including roads, telecommunications, rail lines, and ports. Considerable attention was being focused on rebuilding the old "corridors" to the sea, which had served parts of South Africa, and land-locked countries to the northwest.

From 1992 until 1997, real GDP rose by an average of 7.5% per year. Inflation fell below 6 % in 1998. The country remained highly indebted (external debt was about 3.7 times GDP and about 13 times exports), but debt service was projected to fall to manageable levels.[72] Foreign aid amounted to around two-thirds of GDP.

Foreign investment began to return, especially from Portugal, the former colonial power. Much was for the acquisition of state-owned assets, as the government privatized more than 900 (of about 1,000) entities that it had built or nationalized earlier. Investment from the country's richer neighbor, South Africa, also began to grow as stability returned to Mozambique. Before the peace accords, approved investments numbered about 20 per year. Immediately following the accords, in 1993 thirty-one projects were approved, with a value of $71 million. Since then, foreign investment has steadily grown, as shown in table 2.

Yet, the average size of project (except in 1997 when the Mozal approval was recorded) has remained quite small, at around US$2 million. Clearly, Mozambique was not attracting many large invest-

Table 2. Growth of Foreign Investment since 1993

Year	Number of Projects Approved	Value (in thousands of US$)
1993	20	71,186
1994	130	446,561
1995	166	279,020
1996	270	519,096
1997	184	1,754,318[a]
1998	202	837,834

Source: Figures provided by the Investment Promotion Center.
a. 1997 includes more than US$1.3 million for Mozal.

ments of major multinational enterprises. Yet, by 1998 a number of large investments from well-known multinational enterprises were under discussion. In addition to Billiton's Mozal project, discussions were underway with Enron, ARCO, and Sasol, for example.

Appendix 2
The Aluminum Smelting Process

A luminum is produced from alumina, which in turn comes from bauxite, an ore containing aluminum hydroxide. Leading bauxite producers are Australia, Guinea, Brazil, and Jamaica. About 2.65 tons of bauxite can be converted into one ton of alumina by a chemical process. About 2 tons of alumina can be converted into one ton of aluminum metal in an electrolytic smelting operation. The process is one of electrolysis. In the potline area of the smelter, a huge "pot" serves as a cathode. Anodes are installed above the pot. The pot is filled with alumina and chemicals. A current is passed through and the aluminum particles from the alumina are attracted to the pot, as cathode, and the oxygen is attracted towards the anode.

The aluminum accumulated in the bottom of the pot is transported to the casthouse, where it is kept liquid inside furnaces. It is poured into moulds to form ingots of a standard 22.5 kg each. The ingots are then shipped, in one-ton "packages," to customers, who then fabricate it by rolling, extruding, or casting operations.

The anodes are consumed in the process and have to be replaced regularly. New anodes are manufactured on site, in the carbon plant, from petroleum coke, pitch, and recycled anodes.[73]

The electrolysis process requires large amounts of direct current. The power is received at the smelter as high-voltage alternating current and transformed in a local substation to the direct current required for electrolysis and to forms meeting other energy needs of the project. The cost of electricity is the critical element in making a particular smelter cost competitive.

Since large volumes of alumina have to be imported and large amounts of aluminum must be exported, an aluminum smelter located away from mines and markets has to have access to a port and transport between the port and the smelter.

Appendix 3
Red-tape Study

The FIAS 1996 study of bureaucratic barriers to foreign direct investment in Mozambique[74] divided barriers into four categories: general approval and registration (summarized in figures 5 and 6), site development (example in figure 7), major operating and trading licenses (example in figure 8), and operational requirements. Specific industries required additional steps to those that faced all investors. The report recommended changing legislation and regulations, rationalizing the processes by which legislation and regulations are implemented, and lowering fees. The report suggested that progress could be made under the existing legislation by eliminating duplicate steps in the process, reducing the number of trips to notaries and registries, and eliminating steps not explicitly required by laws and regulations and that are not absolutely essential.

FIGURE 3
Mozambique: Setting Up a New Company

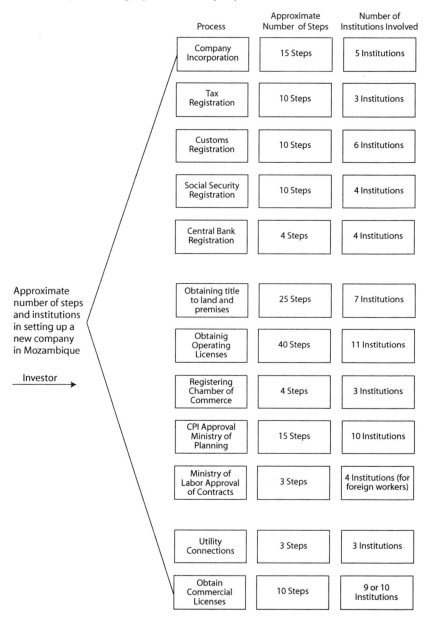

Process	Approximate Number of Steps	Number of Institutions Involved
Company Incorporation	15 Steps	5 Institutions
Tax Registration	10 Steps	3 Institutions
Customs Registration	10 Steps	6 Institutions
Social Security Registration	10 Steps	4 Institutions
Central Bank Registration	4 Steps	4 Institutions
Obtaining title to land and premises	25 Steps	7 Institutions
Obtainig Operating Licenses	40 Steps	11 Institutions
Registering Chamber of Commerce	4 Steps	3 Institutions
CPI Approval Ministry of Planning	15 Steps	10 Institutions
Ministry of Labor Approval of Contracts	3 Steps	4 Institutions (for foreign workers)
Utility Connections	3 Steps	3 Institutions
Obtain Commercial Licenses	10 Steps	9 or 10 Institutions

Approximate number of steps and institutions in setting up a new company in Mozambique

Investor

Source: FIAS, *Mozambique, Administrative Barriers,* op. cit., page 4.

FIGURE 4
Mozambique: Steps Required for a New Company

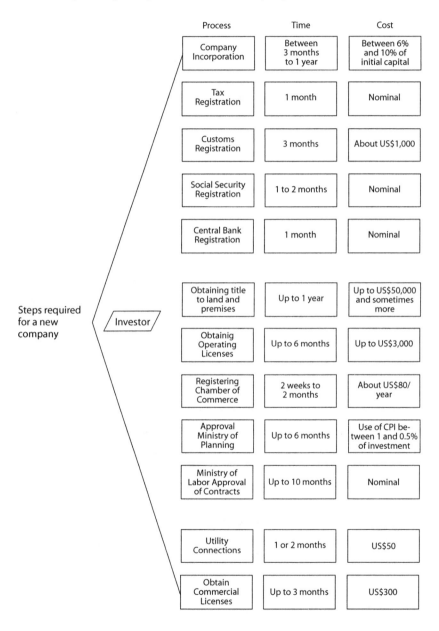

	Process	Time	Cost
Investor	Company Incorporation	Between 3 months to 1 year	Between 6% and 10% of initial capital
	Tax Registration	1 month	Nominal
	Customs Registration	3 months	About US$1,000
	Social Security Registration	1 to 2 months	Nominal
	Central Bank Registration	1 month	Nominal
	Obtaining title to land and premises	Up to 1 year	Up to US$50,000 and sometimes more
	Obtainig Operating Licenses	Up to 6 months	Up to US$3,000
	Registering Chamber of Commerce	2 weeks to 2 months	About US$80/year
	Approval Ministry of Planning	Up to 6 months	Use of CPI between 1 and 0.5% of investment
	Ministry of Labor Approval of Contracts	Up to 10 months	Nominal
	Utility Connections	1 or 2 months	US$50
	Obtain Commercial Licenses	Up to 3 months	US$300

Steps required for a new company

Source: FIAS, *Mozambique, Administrative Barriers,* op. cit., page 5.

FIGURE 5
Mozambique: Steps for a Construction Permit and Property Title

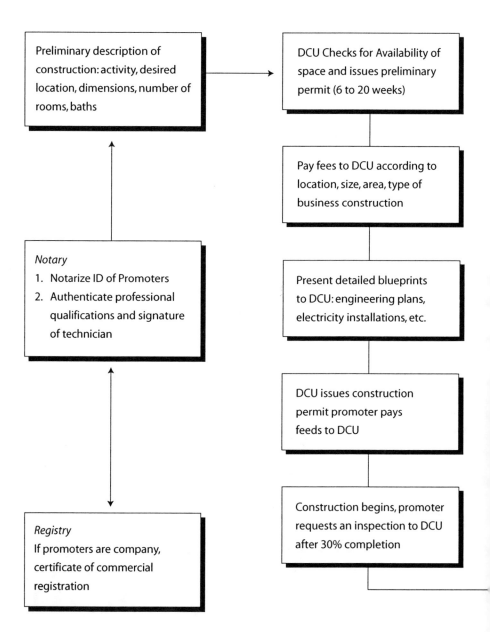

Direccao de Construccao e Urbanismo (DCU) of the Municipal Council
(6 Months to 2 Years; Cost: US$50,000 for Commercial Building)

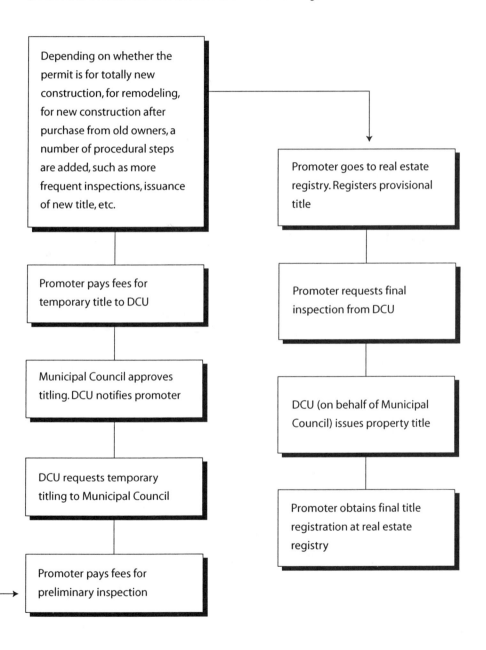

Depending on whether the permit is for totally new construction, for remodeling, for new construction after purchase from old owners, a number of procedural steps are added, such as more frequent inspections, issuance of new title, etc.

Promoter goes to real estate registry. Registers provisional title

Promoter pays fees for temporary title to DCU

Promoter requests final inspection from DCU

Municipal Council approves titling. DCU notifies promoter

DCU (on behalf of Municipal Council) issues property title

DCU requests temporary titling to Municipal Council

Promoter obtains final title registration at real estate registry

Promoter pays fees for preliminary inspection

FIGURE 6
Mozambique: Steps for Obtaining an Industrial License
(between 10 weeks to 1 year)

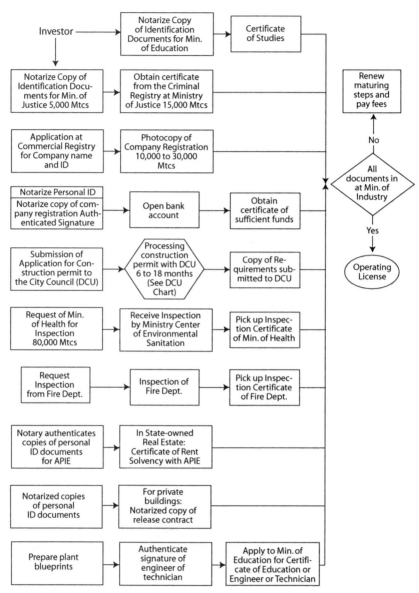

Source: FIAS, *Mozambique, Administrative Barriers,* op. cit., page 57.

Notes

1. Appendix I provides a brief description of Mozambique.

2. World Economic Forum, *The Africa Competitiveness Report: 1998* (Geneva: World Economic Forum, 1998), page 10.

3. Ibid, Tables 2.08, 2.09, 2.12, and 2.17, pages 187–192.

4. Although the findings are described as noted in The Economist Intelligence Unit, *Mozambique Country Report*, 2nd Quarter 1997, page 11, presumably the "70 organizations" are not necessarily 70 *different* organizations. Some of the permits and authorizations are likely issued by the same organization. For the original study on which the business report drew, see FIAS, *Mozambique, Administrative Barriers to Investment: The Red Tape Analysis* (Washington: International Finance Corporation: 1996).

5. These were initially sponsored by multilateral and bilateral donors, but gradually became nearly self-financing through fees from participants.

6. One result was the birth of CTA, the Working Group of Business Associations, which lobbied for reform.

7. FIAS is a joint service of the International Finance Corporation and the World Bank that helps developing countries improve their foreign investment policies.

8. Summarized in *Second Private Sector Conference in Mozambique* (Maputo: Ministry of Industry, Commerce, and Tourism, 1996), pages 35–38, of the English-language section.

9. FIAS, *Mozambique, Administrative Barriers to Investment*, op. cit.
Sample charts from this study are reproduced in Appendix III of this paper.

10. The preparation of Action Plans continued. The schedule for June
1999, for example, called for: 1. revision of the stamp taxes and 2. modern-
ization of notary services. Responsibility for each task was assigned to an
individual, by name.

11. *Third Private Sector Conference in Mozambique* (Maputo: Ministry
of Industry, Commerce, and Tourism, 1997), "Annex I: Progress Report of
the Inter-ministerial Working Group on Removal of Administrative Barriers to Investment," pages 73–75; and Oldemiro Baloi, "Progress Report
on Removing Administrative Barriers to Investment: 1997/98," in *Fourth
Private Sector Conference in Mozambique* (Maputo: Ministry of Industry,
Commerce, and Tourism, 1998), pages 13–15.

12. According to interviews in the Investment Promotion Center.

13. The story was to grow more complicated. In 1998, when it seemed
that Enron's rights had expired, the minister proposed returning some rights
to Sasol. Enron objected publicly, claiming that the minister's decision was
based on personal interests. Relations between Enron and the tutelary ministry deteriorated and the deal seemed blocked for the time being. Enron
did eventually obtain rights to the field, but by June 1999 it still had not
completed a heads of agreement. Many people we interviewed argued that
the re-assignment to Enron was the result of international pressure. When
the rights were returned to Sasol, Enron sought the backing of the U.S.
embassy; moreover, some members of the U.S. Congress seemed to re-
spond to Enron by linking foreign assistance to Mozambique to Enron's
receiving the contract; and U.S. President Clinton was said to have pressed
Mozambique on behalf of Enron in negotiations for a bilateral investment
treaty between the United States and Mozambique. In 1999, tensions over
Enron were still high among many officials we interviewed. For parts of the
story, see: Simon Barber, "Minister Denies Pande Claims," *Business Day*,
December 3, 1998; Charles Mangwiro, "Mozambique in New U.S. Talks
over Natural Gas Fields," *Daily Mail and Guardian*, March 8, 1999.

14. Gencor conducted negotiations in Mozambique through Alusaf Ltd.
(South Africa), its 100%-owned subsidiary, which actually held the smelters
at Richards Bay. In 1994 Gencor had acquired Billiton, a minerals company

that had previously been owned by Royal Dutch Shell. In 1997 Gencor combined its base metals operations, including aluminum, under the internationally known Billiton name. Thus, the project promoter and major investor became Billiton plc, a company listed on the London Stock Exchange.

15. In the past, the aluminum industry had been very concentrated. In 1960, for example, six firms held 77% of the Western world's smelting capacity; in 1965, they held 85% of bauxite mining and 89% of alumina production. See Louis T. Wells, "Minerals: Eroding Oligopolies," in David Yoffie (editor), *Beyond Free Trade: Firms, Governments, and Global Competition* (Boston: Harvard Business School Press, 1993), page 389. The concentration had gradually declined in the 1970s and 1980s as Japanese firms expanded output and new sources of technology and markets allowed state-owned firms in developing countries to enter the industry. With the collapse of the Soviet Union, Eastern European smelters had increasingly entered Western markets.

16. Prices had reached a high of US$3,600 per ton in 1988.

17. One line of 288 reduction pots instead of two lines.

18. For a brief description of the smelting process, see Appendix II.

19. In many cases, as with this project, the alumina comes from an affiliate of the smelter. Whether the parties are affiliated or not, smelting may be done on a "tolling" basis or with a transfer of ownership. Under a tolling arrangement, ownership of the alumina never passes to the smelting company; rather, a fee is simply paid to the smelter for its processing of the alumina for its owner. Alternatively, when ownership is transferred, some price must be established for the alumina. In fact, there is no meaningful published price for alumina. Therefore, the transfer is usually priced as a percentage of the published aluminum price. Of course, where affiliates are involved, neither a fee nor a transfer price is likely to be arm's length.

20. Maputo was only about 95 km from the South African border. Before the Mozambican civil war, Maputo had served as an important port for goods moving to and from the northeastern part of South Africa.

21. The Richards Bay electricity was purchased under a contract from Eskom. Eskom's existing contracts guaranteed certain users the lowest price offered by Eskom to any customer inside South Africa. The contracts did not, however, require Eskom to lower these prices if it offered a lower price

for electricity to a customer outside South Africa. Thus, Mozal was able to cut a favorable deal for electricity for a new smelter in Mozambique.

22. Raw material costs amounted to about 40%, but differed little from smelter to smelter.

23. The lines would cost about $100 million, an amount included in the estimated project cost. Some otherwise attractive sites in South Africa, such as the Cape Town area, were considered as too distant from low-cost power.

24. The partners would seek to obtain the balance of the equity from metal traders and potential customers. The rest of the financing would, it was hoped, be supplied under a mix of subordinated debt and senior debt.

25. Reid had worked with Oberholzer to bring the Hillside smelting project on line. Should the new smelter materialize, Reid would likely become the Managing Director of the project.

26. The investment was larger than published GDP at that time.

27. Estimated in an evaluation conducted for the IFC and reported in J. Berns, "Specialist Study-S7: Assessment of the Socio-Economic Impact of Alusaf's Proposed Aluminium Smelter in Maputo, Mozambique," CSIR Environmentek, Pretoria, July 1996, revised November 1996.

28. The only other very large project that was under construction was a toll road, being built by South African investors, from the South African border to Maputo. Mozambicans explained that this was a rather special case. The agreement for the road was the product of close relations between South Africa's post-apartheid government and Mozambican officials, a relationship that had developed in the days when Mozambique was a "front-line state" in the battle against apartheid in South Africa. Moreover, agreements for a smelter were to be much more complicated and involve many more parties.

29. The company name was actually Mozal SARL, but we will refer to both the project and the company as Mozal throughout this paper.

30. For a fuller explanation of why ministry-by-ministry negotiations lead to a sub-optimal outcome, see Dennis J. Encarnation and Louis T. Wells, "Sovereignty en Garde: Negotiating with Foreign Investors," *International Organization*, Vol. 39, No. 1 (Winter 1985), pp. 47–78.

31. These included the ministers of Industry, Commerce, and Tourism; Coordination of Environmental Affairs; Planning and Finance; Public Works and Housing; and Mineral Resources and Energy.

32. The degree of optimism, and also a certain degree of naiveté, are reflected in the date proposed by the company's target for an agreement, November 1996, and for a go-ahead decision, March 1997. To speed things along, Oberholzer proposed in the next week that the Ministry of Industry, Commerce, and Tourism issue a ministerial directive to all departments concerned to ensure that the managers could "avoid difficulties in arranging appointments or discussing solutions and then having the appointments ignored." This directive was never sent.

33. The names of parts of the structure changed over time, as did the make-up. We have chosen to use the names that had become standard by mid-1999.

34. The Investment Promotion Center reported to the Ministry of Planning and Finance. Thus, the Center's member represented the ministry, as well.

35. From minutes of the first meeting, on May 29, 1996.

36. Quoted from the minutes of the first meeting, on May 29, 1996.

37. Under "Regulations on Industrial Free Zones," approved by Decree No. 18/93, of 14th September 1993, with changes approved by Decree No. 38/93, of 8th August 1995.

38. The regulations (Article 46, "Regulamento de Zonas Francas Industriais em Moçambique," approved under Decreto no 38/95, de 08 Agosto) for industrial free zones called for one of three different taxes, in lieu of income and dividends taxes: 1% of turnover, US$0.75 per square meter of land per month, or US$19 per square meter of land per year. The investor was to state a preference in his application.

39. The investment law gave all approved foreign investment a broad exemption from exchange controls.

40. In order to convince customs officials that such a system could work, and to learn more details about how other countries handled the problems associated with free-trade zones, the Investment Promotion Center eventually (in September–October 1998) sponsored visits by some members of the GLC to Mauritius, Malaysia, the Philippines, and the Dominican Republic to look at free-trade zones and the governing legislation and regulations in action. Very helpful in this was J. Ceron, a resident advisor stationed in the Investment Promotion Center. He was from the Dominican Republic and that country's model became especially influential in the design of arrangements in Mozambique.

41. The toll road, mentioned in an earlier note, was under construction by a South African-French consortium to improve traffic flow between Maputo and South Africa. This was part of a broader plan to rebuild the so-called Maputo Corridor connecting Johannesburg with the harbor at Maputo.

42. Company managers pointed out that the company would have to bear the interest cost on the "loan," amounting to some $18 million over the eight-year repayment period.

43. The agreed fiscal terms and other provisions governing the Mozal project are contained in the Memorandum of Understanding ("Acordo de Princípios: Mozal-Projecto de Fundição"), March 20, 1997, and in the annexes included in Resolução Interna No/97, November 1997, approving the project by the Council of Ministers.

44. The company provided transport to Richards Bay, via its corporate plane. The flight was less than one hour from Maputo. Company management viewed these trips as an important incentive to attendance by government officials, who were provided opportunities for shopping in South Africa.

45. See an earlier note for description of corporate changes involving Gencor.

46. For more information on the financing of Mozal, see Benjamin Esty, "Financing the Mozal Project," Harvard Business School case, N9-200-005, 1999.

47. The alumina and aluminum were to be transported between the port and the smelter by truck, although a rail line existed near the smelter site. CFM management believed that the volume of trucking required (an estimate was one truck per hour day and night) would eventually lead the company to prefer rail, where it would also have a role.

48. With 18,000 employees.

49. Water issues are of particular importance in Mozambique as the country has a very limited supply of drinkable water and is prone to drought. This subsequently became a very serious issue in the discussions relating to Enron's iron and steel project, which would require a large amount of water.

50. Ceron had experience with other negotiations in his earlier job with the Dominican Republic's investment promotion agency, in his home country.

51. Macamo took over in May 1998, following the death of Moiane.

52. For information on linkage programs elsewhere, see Joseph Battat, Isaiah Frank, and Xiaofang Shen, *Suppliers to Multinationals: Linkage Programs to Strengthen Local Companies in Developing Countries* (Washington: FIAS, 1996).

53. CPI was usually able to pay per-diem for officials travelling to Richards Bay. No extra compensation had been provided to officials for attendance at the meetings of other groups.

54. *Mozal News*, March 1999.

55. The duty and sales tax on the normal import of construction materials usually amounted to about 12% of the value.

56. For descriptions of various ways of structuring participation of ministries, see Dennis J. Encarnation and Louis T. Wells, op. cit., and Louis T Wells and Alvin G. Wint, *Facilitating Foreign Investment: Government Institutions to Screen, Monitor and Service Investment from Abroad*, FIAS Occasional Paper no. 2, 1991.

57. This gain is partly negated by the terms that were eventually negotiated to allow the company to write off part of its expenditure on infrastructure open to the public. This is not called for in the IFZ law; on the other hand, one could argue that the government should pay for public infrastructure, and that the company is simply financing this expenditure for the government.

58. The pattern is labeled as the "obsolescing bargain" in some literature. See, for example, Raymond Vernon, *Sovereignty at Bay* (New York: Basic Books, 1971), Chapter 2.

59. In 1999, two oil company executives were quoted in the *New York Times* as calling for renegotiations of their contracts in Venezuela, in response to low oil prices. The president of Shell de Venezuela, according to the article, said "that foreign oil companies here are in an 'unsustainable' situation and suggested a renegotiation of contracts might be in order." A Conoco executive was quoted, ". . . you can expect Conoco will visit with the Venezuelans about fine-tuning the terms . . . " Both of these statements appeared in the *New York Times*, April 17, 1999, page B14. There are many other examples of renegotiations to favor investors. Two, the 1986 renegotiation of Bougainville Copper and 1994–1998 renegotiations of BP's pe-

troleum agreement in Colombia, are cited in Thomas Waelde and Abba Kolo, "Renegotiation and Contract Adaption in the International Investment Projects: Applicable Legal Principles & Industry Practices," *The CEPMLP Journal*, Volume 5-3a, http://w.w.w.dundee.ac.uk/cepmplp/html/article5-4a.htm, n.d.

60. By the time of our interviews, a Task Force had been formed for the Maputo Iron and Steel Project, under the Minister of Mineral Resources and Energy as chairman. It was, however, not meeting on a regular basis. As of June 1999, Enron had no team in residence that could provide the equivalent of MOZAL's resident management group to work with a second-tier Government Liaison Committee.

61. For the importance of this function in an investment promotion program, see Louis T. Wells, "Revisiting *Marketing a Country: Promotion as a Tool for Attracting Foreign Investment*," forthcoming from FIAS, 2000.

62. This new ministry resulted from a division of activities of the previous Ministry of Industry, Commerce, and Tourism.

63. For this latter rating, see: Jeffrey D. Sachs and Sara E. Severs, "Executive Summary," from *The Africa Competitiveness Report*, http://www.ksg. harvard.edu/cid/acr98exec.pdf.

64. This was the typical pattern in Indonesia under Suharto, for example, where investors regularly went directly to the president, his family, or close associates to resolve problems. As a result, inter-ministerial groups established to deal with business problems typically deteriorated, as members became demoralized and stopped regular attendance at meetings.

65. For an early description that classifies multinational enterprises in terms of their "personalities" in connection with government relations (in this case, willingness to intervene in local politics), see Charles Goodsell, *American Corporations and Peruvian Politics* (Cambridge: Harvard University Press, 1974).

66. Another company that was considering a project in Mozambique had established a reputation of using its home government to apply pressure to the top levels of the Mozambican government. It would have provided a less attractive candidate for the liaison experiment than Mozal.

67. This step has not always been taken elsewhere. In the now well-known case of Intel in Costa Rica, the inter-ministerial structures devel-

oped to attract Intel did not survive the one effort. For the story of attracting Intel, see Debora Spar, *Attracting High Technology Investment: Intel's Costa Rica Plant* (Washington: Foreign Investment Advisory Service, 1998).

68. In December of 1999, Mozambique successfully held its second democratic elections. Frelimo won the new elections and President Chissano was elected to another five-year term. When the president appointed his new cabinet, Minister Baloi, who had been vocal about his desire to leave government service, was not included in the new lineup. He has since taken on the role of "Administrador" for the Mozal project.

69. As noted, Baloi chaired the Inter-ministerial Working Group to Remove Administrative Barriers to Investment and had played a major role in the Private Sector Conferences.

70. Estimated figure reported in Job Rabkin, "Mozambique: Devastated by Civil War," FT.com, Special Reports: IMF/World Bank, http://www.ft.com/specials98/q 3632.htm.

71. World Economic Forum, *The Africa Competitiveness Report: 1998* (Geneva: World Economic Forum, 1998).

72. Mozambique was eligible for the IMF and World Bank's Highly Indebted Poor Country (HIPC) initiative and was granted significant debt relief in July of 1999.

73. For Mozal, liquid pitch could be supplied by road tanker from South Africa. About 92,000 tons per year of petroleum coke would come from the suppliers to Hillside, but it would be imported through Maputo.

74. FIAS, *Mozambique, Administrative Barriers to Investment: The Red Tape Analysis* (Washington: International Finance Corporation: 1996).